212 VICTORY POEMS

212 VICTORY POEMS

Compiled and Written

by

CLIFFORD LEWIS

Evangelist, Youth Leader and World Traveler,
Author of *Japan Needs Jesus, Thrills of Christian
Youth, Youth on the March, God's Ideal Woman,*
and *Will Revival Come Before Christ Comes?*

ZONDERVAN   PUBLISHING   HOUSE
GRAND RAPIDS, MICHIGAN

Eight-fifteen Franklin Street
Grand Rapids, Michigan

INTRODUCTION

MANY OF THE POEMS in this book have been used in my evangelistic campaigns, radio programs, youth conferences, high school and college chapel services throughout America and also on the evangelistic and missionary tour around the world. They were selected, not because of literary merit from a critical standpoint, but because they have a message and heart appeal. Some were sent to me by friends and for several years I have gleaned poems from many sources.

I wish to express my sincere appreciation to those whose poems are used in this collection. I have tried to trace the ownership of copyrighted poems and have done my best to secure all necessary permission from authors or their authorized agents, or from both. I have been unable to find out the authors of every poem but I am sure that they will be thankful that the Lord is using their testimony. I always rejoice to have my poems used by any of God's servants. I will be pleased, upon notification of any error, to make proper acknowledgment in future editions of this book.

Some of my friends are very anxious to help circulate these poems throughout the world. The book will be used for gifts on various occasions. They will be sent to missionaries in many lands. I am praying that through the reading of these poems sinners will be converted, Christians strengthened and encouraged, young people inspired, and the sick and shut-ins comforted.

I am always glad to receive from those who read my books their testimonies, prayer requests, inspirational poems, helpful mottoes, outlines and illustrations, which I can pass on to others.

—*Clifford Lewis*
Bob Jones College,
Cleveland, Tennessee.

CONTENTS

THE BIBLE

MY BIBLE AND I

"We've traveled together, my Bible and I,
   Through all kinds of weather, with smile or with sigh!
In sorrow or sunshine, in tempest or calm!
   Thy friendship unchanging, my lamp and my psalm.

We've traveled together, my Bible and I
   When life had grown weary, and death e'en was nigh!
But all through the darkness of mist or of wrong,
   I found there a solace, a prayer, and a song.

So now who shall part us, my Bible and I?
   Shall 'isms' or schisms, or 'new lights' who try?
Shall shadow for substance, or stone for good bread,
   Supplant thy sound wisdom, give folly instead?

Ah, no, my dear Bible, exponent of light!
   Thou sword of the Spirit, put error to flight!
And still through life's journey, until my last sigh,
   We'll travel together, my Bible and I."

GOD'S WORD

God's Holy Word has surely been
   Inspired of God, and not of men;
No power nor eloquence of man
   Could e'er conceive its wondrous plan.

Withstanding all the tests of time,
   It stands unchanged, unique, sublime,
Proving to every tongue and race
   God's wisdom, mercy, love, and grace.

All efforts to destroy are vain—
   God's Holy Word will still remain;
So hammer on, ye hostile hands,
   Your hammers break; God's Anvil stands.

M. E. H.

"I KNOW THE BOOK IS TRUE"

"O the precious, precious Bible,
  God's messenger of love,
Ever lifting fallen man-kind
  To a higher plane above;
'Tis a lamp unto my pathway
  Tho' old yet ever new,
I'm acquainted with the author,
  And I know the Book is true.

Each time I search its pages
  New treasures rare I find,
How the blessed, loving Saviour
  Cures sickness of all kind;
'Tis a message of salvation
  To the Gentile and the Jew,
I'm acquainted with the author,
  And I know the Book is true.

I know some people doubt it,
  This precious Book divine,
But I couldn't do without it,
  I believe it, line for line;
'Tis the very same sweet Gospel
  That my dear old mother knew,
Get acquainted with the author,
  And you'll know the Book is true."

MY BIBLE

"This Holy Book I'd rather own
    Than all the gold and gems,
That e'er in monarch's coffers shone
    Than all their diadems.

Nay, were the seas one chrysolite,
    The earth one golden ball,
And diamonds all the stars of night,
    This Book outweighs them all.

Ah, no, the soul ne'er found relief
    In glittering hoards of wealth;
Gems dazzle not the eye of grief,
    Gold cannot purchase health.

But here a blessed balm appears
　To heal the deepest woe;
And those who read this Book in tears
　Their tears shall cease to flow.

Thou truest friend man ever knew
　Thy constancy I have tried;
When all were false I found thee true,
　My counselor and guide.

The mines of earth no treasures give
　That can this volume buy;
In teaching me the way to live
　It has taught me how to die."

READ THE BIBLE THROUGH

I supposed I knew the Bible,
Reading piece-meal, hit or miss;
Now a bit of John or Matthew,
Now a snatch of Genesis.

Certain chapters of Isaiah,
Certain Psalms—the twenty-third!
Twelfth of Romans, first of Proverbs.
Yes, I thought I knew the Word!

But I found that thorough reading
Was a different thing to do,
And the way was unfamiliar
When I read the Bible through.

You who like to play at Bible,
Dip and dabble, here and there,
Just before you kneel aweary,
And yawn through a hurried prayer.

You who treat the Crown of Writings,
As you treat no other book,—
Just a paragraph disjointed,
Just a crude, impatient look.

Try a worthier procedure,
Try a broad and steady view;
You will kneel in very rapture
When you read the Bible through.

—*Amos R. Wells*

THE WORD OF GOD

"The word of our God shall stand forever."—Isa. 40:8

Though heart grows faint and spirits sink,
 By every wind of feeling blown;
Though faith itself may seem to fail,
 I rest upon Thy word alone.

That word of power that framed the worlds,
 Unfailing, changeless, strong, and sure.
Though heaven and earth should pass away,
 What Thou hast spoken must endure.

Is Thine arm shortened, Thine ear dulled?
 What Thou hast sworn hast Thou forgot?
God of the everlasting years,
 All else may fail; Thou failest not.

Against the foeman's fiery darts
 I wield anew the Spirit's sword,
And answer every fresh assault
 With ever-fresh "Thus saith the Lord."

And, when some promised blessing seems
 Too great, too wonderful for me,
I dare by faith to call it mine,
 With "It is written" all my plea.

'Mid shifting sands of doubt and fear
 This is the one foundation-stone;
My soul hath cast her anchor here;
 I rest upon Thy word alone.

—*Annie Johnson Flint*

The Bible Stands

"The Bible stands like a rock undaunted
    'Mid the raging storms of time;
Its pages burn with truth eternal
    And they glow with a light sublime.

The Bible stands like a towering mountain
    Above the works of men;
Its truth by none can be refuted,
    And destroy it, they never can.

The Bible stands and it will forever
    When the world has passed away;
By inspiration it has been given,
    All its precepts I'll obey.

The Bible stands every test we give it,
    For its author is Divine,
By grace alone I hope to live it
    And prove it, and make it mine."

His Word Is Powerful

His Word is like fire consuming,
    His Word is a hammer to break;
His Word is a sword with two edges,
    His Word like a lamp you can take.

His Word is against the false prophets,
    His Word is opposed to all sin;
His Word will endure forever,
    His Word will the victory win.

His Word is both written and living,
    His Word will outlive sword and pen;
His Word is His eternal edict,
    His Word:—it is yea and amen.

—H. H. Savage

A Home Without a Bible

"What is a home without a Bible?
    'Tis a home where day is night,
Starless night, for on life's pathway
    Heaven can shed no kindly light.

What is a home without a Bible?
　'Tis a place where daily bread
For the body is provided,
　But the soul is never fed.

What is a home without a Bible?
　'Tis a family out at sea,
Compass lost and rudder broken
　Drifting, drifting, hopelessly.

What is a home without a Bible?
　List and ponder while I speak,
'Tis a home with a Bible in it,
　But not opened once a week.

Lost! the Bible—lost! its teachings,
　Lost! Its help each day in seven;
Lost! To live by—lost! to die by,
　Lost! What's lost? The way to Heaven!"

THE GOSPEL ACCORDING TO YOU

"There's a sweet old story translated for man,
　But writ in the long, long ago,
The Gospel according to Mark, Luke, and John,
　Of Christ and His mission below.

You are writing a gospel, a chapter each day,
　By deeds that you do, by words that you say,
Men read what you write, whether faithless or true—
　Say, what is the gospel according to you?

'Tis a wonderful story, that gospel of love,
　As it shines in the Christ-life divine,
And oh, that its truth might be told again
　In the story of your life and mine.

Unselfishness mirrors in every scene,
　Love blossoms on every sod,
And back from its vision the heart comes to tell
　The wonderful goodness of God.

You are writing each day a letter to men
　Take care that the writing is true;
'Tis the only gospel some men will read,
　That gospel according to you."

"THE WORLD'S BIBLE"

Christ has no hands but our hands
   To do His work today;
He has no feet but our feet
   To lead men in His way;
He has no tongue but our tongue
   To tell men how He died;
He has no help but our help
   To bring them to His side.

We are the only Bible
   The careless world will read;
We are the sinners gospel,
   We are the scoffer's creed;
We are the Lord's last message,
   Given in deed and word;
What if the type is crooked?
   What if the print is blurred?

What if our hands are busy
   With other work than His?
What if our feet are walking
   Where sin's allurement is?
What if our tongues are speaking
   Of things His lips would spurn?
How can we hope to help Him
   And hasten His return?

—Annie Johnson Flint

(Copyright by Evangelical Publishers, Toronto, Canada)

AN OLD-FASHIONED PREACHER

"How dear to my heart is the church of my childhood
   Where I took my first step in the straight, narrow way;
The little white church near the thick-tangled wildwood
   Where I went with my mother on each Sabbath day.
There was no large pipe-organ, no high-paid soprano;
   The singing was scarcely the best ever heard;
But the man in the pulpit, divinely commissioned,
   Poured out his whole soul in proclaiming God's Word.
An old-fashioned preacher, a real Bible preacher,
   A spirit-filled preacher who honored the Word.

How thrilling it was just to see him in action,
　This soldier of Christ, with his keen, trusty 'sword,'
Who wielded his weapon with zeal and devotion,
　And backed up each thrust with a 'Thus saith the Lord!'
No uncertain sound ever came from his trumpet,
　His hearers were moved—yes, convicted and stirred;
And, bowing the knee in wet-eyed confession,
　Accepted the truth as revealed in the Word,
By this old-fashioned preacher, this full Gospel preacher,
　This spirit-taught preacher who honored the Word.

Sometimes, when I list to the ramifications
　Of science, that twist my poor brain out of shape,
Or hear the consensus of scholarship's findings,
　Regarding our old friend, the anthropoid ape;
As my mind reels, confused with drives, plans, and programs,
　And world federations toward which we are stirred—
Sociology, politics, internationalism,
　I sigh for the sermons my infancy heard,
From this old-fashioned preacher, this soul-stirring preacher,
　This heart-warming preacher who honored God's Word."

CHRIST

While conducting a young people's revival in Atlanta, Georgia, in June of 1930, I wrote this poem after climbing the famous Stone Mountain:

JESUS CHRIST THE ROCK OF AGES

As I sit on top of this mountain,
  Hundreds of feet in the air,
I feel the wind blowing gently,
  I gaze at the sky, and it's fair.

I think of the beauties of nature,
  Of the God who made them all,
Of rivers, mountains, and forests,
  Of the rills and the great waterfall.

My thoughts wander back through the ages,
  To Greece, to Babylon, and Rome,
To Pompeii with all of her splendor,
  And then to my childhood home.

Away out there in the country
  Far from the busy throng,
I didn't hear much of this world,
  But I heard an old sweet song.

Out there we had little of money
  With which to put on "airs,"
Thank God we had something better,
  We had mother's earnest prayers.

Now she has gone on to Heaven,
  That blessed home in the sky;
Thank God for the glorious promise,
  We shall meet in the sweet bye and bye.

There in that home eternal,
  Beside the golden shore,
With mother, the angels, and Jesus
  I'll dwell for evermore.

17

The flowers and grass of this mountain
    Will wither and soon fade away,
But the flowers of Heaven are fadeless,
    And they bloom through endless day.

The wind and the rain cut this mountain,
    Their marks can be seen everywhere;
But in Heaven the storms are forgotten,
    No tempest to trouble us there.

Lo, the sun is hid from my vision,
    And soon come the shadows of night;
In Heaven we'll never have darkness,
    For Jesus, God's Son, is the light.

The walls of this mountain are granite,
    As great as earth's walls can be;
But in glory the walls are of jasper
    That surround the silvery sea.

Some day this old rock will vanish,
    Will crumble and fall away;
But Jesus, the Rock of Ages,
    Will live and reign for aye.

Friend, are you standing firmly,
    On Jesus, your all in all?
Worldly rocks may stand for a moment,
    But some day they'll surely fall.

Your feet may not seem to be slipping
    As you see not the danger that waits;
But in Jesus you're safe forever
    And bound for Heaven's pearly gates.

Oh, why not trust this dear Savior?
    Accept Him without delay,
Say, "Jesus, save me, a sinner,"
    And He'll cleanse and save you today.

                              —Clifford Lewis

CHRIST

Christ for sickness, Christ for health,
Christ for poverty, Christ for wealth,
Christ for joy, Christ for sorrow,
Christ today, and Christ tomorrow;
Christ my Life, and Christ my Light,
Christ for morning, noon and night;
Christ when all around gives way,
Christ my everlasting stay;
Christ my rest, Christ my food,
Christ above my highest good;
Christ my well beloved, my Friend,
Christ my pleasure without end;
Christ my Savior, Christ my Lord,
Christ my portion, Christ my God;
Christ my Shepherd, I His sheep,
Christ himself my soul doth keep;
Christ my Leader, Christ my Peace,
Christ hath brought my soul's release,
Christ my Righteousness divine,
Christ for me, for He is mine;
Christ my Wisdom, Christ my Meat,
Christ restores my wand'ring feet,
Christ my Advocate and Priest,
Christ who ne'er forgets the least;
Christ my Teacher, Christ my Guide,
Christ my Rock, in Christ I hide;
Christ the everlasting Bread,
Christ His precious blood hath shed;
Christ hath brought us near to God,
Christ the everlasting Word,
Christ my Master, Christ my Head,
Christ Who for my sins hath bled;
Christ my Glory, Christ my Crown,
Christ the Plant of great Renown,
Christ my Comforter on high,
Christ my Hope draws ever nigh.

—H. W. S.

THIS IS THE TRUE GOD

The Maker of the universe
As Man for men was made a curse;
The claims of laws that He had made
Unto the uttermost He paid.

His holy fingers formed the bough
Where grew the thorns that crowned His brow;
The nails that pierced His hands were mined
In secret places He designed.

He made the forests whence there sprung
The tree on which His body hung;
He died upon a Cross of wood,
Yet made the hill on which it stood.

The sun which hid from Him its face
By His decree was poised in space;
The skies which darkened o'er His head
By Him above the earth were spread.

The spear which spilt His precious blood
Was tempered in the fires of God;
The grave in which His form was laid
Was hewn in rocks His hands had made.

The throne on which He now appears
Was His from everlasting years;
But a new glory crowns His brow,
And every knee to Him shall bow.

—F. W. Pitt

THAT HE MAY BE GLORIFIED

She was only a simple serving maid
 In a home of idolatry,
What could she do to serve the Lord
 In her lonely captivity?
"If my master would go to the prophet,"
 She said, in all humility,
"He would learn of Jehovah of Israel,
 And be healed of his leprosy."

She was only a simple serving maid,
    Whose faith had been sorely tried,
But God has chosen the things that are naught,
    That HE may be glorified.

He was only a lad from Jerusalem,
    Not specially bad—or good,
But straight to the Master he went and said,
    "Here's my little parcel of food;
It isn't much, but it's all I have,
    My Mother gave it to me;
The loaves are few, and the fishes but two:
    I gladly give them to Thee."

It was only a parcel of food for one,
    But that day it was multiplied,
God has chosen the things that are naught,
    That HE may be glorified.

She was only a humble village maid
    To whom Gabriel came that night,
"Thou art highly favoured of God," he said,
    But she trembled at the sight.
"Fear not," he added, "I bring thee good news,
    A Son shall be born of thee;
The Kingdom of David shall be His right,
    And Jesus His name shall be."

She was only a humble village maid,
    In whom GOD had come to abide,
But HE has chosen the things that are naught,
    That HE may be glorified.

                        —*G. R. H. W.*

HE'S ALTOGETHER LOVELY

He's altogether lovely,
   He is the perfect One;
He's the Lily of the valley,
   Of God and man the Son.

He's altogether lovely,
   Worthy of love and praise;
He's the Lamb without a blemish,
   Oh, honor Him always.

He's altogether lovely,
   He is the open Door;
He's the ever-seeking Shepherd,
   Praise Him forever more!

He's altogether lovely,
   He took my sin and shame;
He's the Fairest of ten thousand,
   Wonderful is His name!

He's altogether lovely,
   Accept Him, He's the Way;
He's the Faithful One and Holy,
   Oh, make Him yours today.

He's altogether lovely,
   His beauty fills my soul;
He's the lovely Rose of Sharon,
   Praise Him while ages roll!

He's altogether lovely,
   He's every day the same;
He's the bright and Morning Star,
   Oh, praise His matchless name!

He's altogether lovely,
   Loud let hosannas ring;
He's the Everlasting Father,
   He is my coming King!

—Helen A. Lewis

I Know He's Mine

"I know not how that Bethlehem's Babe
     Could in the Godhead be;
I only know the manger Child
     Has brought God's life to me.

I know not how that Calvary's Cross
     A world from sin could free;
I only know its matchless love
     Has brought God's love to me.

I know not how that Joseph's tomb
     Could solve death's mystery;
I only know a living Christ,
     Our Immortality."

When I Think of His Love

When I think of the cross where my Savior died,
     'Neath the frown of the darkened skies,
When I hear the groan of the Crucified,
     And I look on those death-closed eyes,
When I know that for me He the anguish bore,
     From sin He might set me free,
Oh, I know that I'll love Him forevermore,
     When I think of His love for me.

When I think of the grave where they laid my Lord,
     And they sealed Him within the gloom,
When I think how according to His Word
     He arose from that vanquished tomb,
Oh, I know that for me He endured it all,
     My eyes with tears grow dim,
While low at His feet in love I fall,
     Whenever I think of Him.

                         —*Louis Paul Lehman, Jr.*
          (Copyrighted by the author)

THE WASHERWOMAN'S FRIEND

"In a very humble cot,
In a rather quiet spot,
In the suds and in the soap
Worked a woman full of hope,
Working, singing all alone
In a sort of undertone,
'With a Savior for a friend,
He will keep me to the end.'

Sometimes happening along,
I have heard the semi-song,
And I often used to smile,
More in sympathy than in guile;
But I never said a word
In regard to what I heard,
As she sang about her friend,
Who would keep her to the end.

Not in sorrow nor in glee,
Working all day long was she,
As her children, three or four,
Played around her on the floor;
But in monotones the song
She was humming all day long,
'With a Savior for a friend,
He will keep me to the end.'

Just a trifle lonesome she,
Just as poor as poor could be;
But her spirits always rose
Like the bubbles in the clothes,
And though widowed and alone,
Cheered her with the monotone
Of a Savior and a friend,
Who would keep her to the end.

I have seen her rub and scrub
On the washboard in the tub,
While the baby, sopped in suds,
Rolled and tumbled in the duds,

Or was paddling in the pools
With old scissors stuck in spools,
She was humming of her friend,
Who would keep her to the end.

Human hopes and human creeds
Have their roots in human needs,
And I would not wish to strip
From that washerwoman's lip
Any song that she can sing,
Any hope that song can bring,
For the woman had a friend,
Who did keep her to the end."

NOT A DISAPPOINTMENT

"He is not a disappointment!
    Jesus is far more to me
Than in all my glowing day-dreams
    I had fancied He could be;
And the more I get to know Him,
    So the more I find Him true,
And the more I long that others
    Should be led to know Him too.

He is not a disappointment!
    He has saved my soul from sin;
All the guilt and all the anguish
    Which oppressed my heart within,
He has banished by His presence;
    And His blessed kiss of peace
Has assured my heart forever
    That His love will never cease.

He is not a disappointment!
    He is all in all to me—
Savior, Sanctifier, Keeper,
    The unchanging Christ is He!
He has won my heart's affections,
    And He meets my every need;
He is not a disappointment,
    For He satisfies indeed."

The Right Choice

To each is given his own free will,
    But remember, if we choose
To follow Christ, we always win,
    If Satan, we always lose.

With his subtle tempting snares,
    The devil seeks to win
Each person in this world below,
    To live a life of sin.

With His tender cords of love,
    Christ draws us one and all,
And as we trust Him day by day
    He'll never let us fall.

Why not say goodby to sin,
    Accept God's gift so free,
Just say in simple, trusting faith,
    "I know He died for me."

When you repent and sins forsake,
    Forgiven you will be,
A child of God you then become
    Because of Calvary.

It always pays to follow Christ,
    Will you not choose today,
To live the more abundant Life,
    And dwell with Him for aye?

In that land of never ending day,
    How thankful you will be,
That you did make the proper choice
    For all eternity.

—Clifford Lewis

"My Lord and I"

I have a friend so precious,
So very dear to me,
He loves me with such tender love,
He loves so faithfully;
I could not live apart from Him,
I love to feel Him nigh,
And so we dwell together,
My Lord and I.

He knows how much I love Him,
He knows I love Him well,
But with what love He loveth me,
My tongue can never tell;
It is an everlasting love,
In ever rich supply,
And so we love each other,
My Lord and I.

Sometimes I'm faint and weary,
He knows that I am weak,
And as He bids me lean on Him,
His help I gladly seek;
He leads me in the paths of light
Beneath a sunny sky,
And so we walk together,
My Lord and I.

I tell Him all my sorrows,
I tell Him all my joys,
I tell Him all that pleases me,
I tell Him what annoys;
He tells me what I ought to do,
He tells me what to try,
And so we talk together,
My Lord and I.

He knows how I am longing
Some weary soul to win,
And so He bids me go and speak
A loving word for Him;
He bids me tell His wondrous love,
And why He came to die,
And so we work together,
My Lord and I.

I have His yoke upon me,
And easy 'tis to bear,
In the burden which He carries
I gladly take a share;
For then it is my happiness
To have Him always nigh,
We bear the yoke together,
My Lord and I.

—*Mrs. L. Shorey*

CHRISTMAS

THE BELLS ON CHRISTMAS DAY

"I heard the bells on Christmas Day
Their old, familiar carols play,
    And wild and sweet
    The words repeat
Of peace on earth, good-will to men!

And thought how, as the day had come,
The belfries of all Christendom
    Had rolled along
    The unbroken song
Of peace on earth, good-will to men!

And in despair I bowed my head;
'There is no peace on earth,' I said;
    'For hate is strong,
    And mocks the song
Of peace on earth, good-will to men!'

Then pealed the bells more loud and deep:
'God is not dead; nor doth He sleep!
    The Wrong shall fail,
    The Right prevail,
With peace on earth, good-will to men!'"

CHRISTMAS

No sheep in the folds,
No star in the west,
No Babe lulled to sleep
On His young mother's breast.
But sheep of God's flock
Straying far from His love,
And a glorified Man
Interceding above.

No gold and no myrrh,
No sweet frankincense,
But the gift of the heart
When the sinner repents.
No music on earth
From the angelic bands;
But the praise and prayer
Of the saved of all lands.

Apart from the Christ—
No joy at his birth,
Though merry and gay
All the feasting on earth;
The candles burn out,
And the feasting is done,
But the Glory of Heaven
Shines forth in God's Son.

—Betty Scott Stam
Yang Chow, China, 1931

THE BRIGHTNESS OF HIS GLORY

The stars of morning that together sang
    Before foundations of the earth were laid
Were listening now; for skies a-sparkle rang
    With song of angels whose glad music made
The drowsy world to wake. That clear, sweet clang
    Of Heaven's opening door would never fade
Upon earth's ear; and it had ne'er been heard
Had not He come, God's own incarnate Word!

The glory with the Father, which was His
    Before the world was made, He laid aside;
Thus gentle Mary to her heart in bliss
    Could press the Child and unto God confide
Her wondering thoughts. She did not know her kiss
    Fell on soft hands that would be crucified—
Small baby palms which held secure between
The mystery of the seven stars, unseen!

E'en angels in high Heaven wished to know
    How bodily in Him—this tiny Child—
The fullness of the Godhead dwelt. And lo!
    To trusting human hearts the Savior mild
Reveals Himself, as softly as the sifted snow
    Falls on tall mountain-tops so bleak and wild;
And Spirit-born, His seeking ones from far
Are guided Home by Bethlehem's glowing star.
                            —*Grace W. Haight*

A CHRISTMAS THOUGHT

Christ Jesus was born in a stable—
    A birthplace of humblest degree,
So that no one could say, "I am poorer,
    More lacking in comforts, than He."

His mother in swaddling bands wrapped Him,
    The wardrobe of One, the Divine,
That no one could say of His raiment,
    "Christ's garments were better than mine."

His home and His comforts were borrowed—
    No pillow for resting His head!
But He lived, and He suffered and sorrowed,
    To give us true comforts instead.

In glory His wealth had been boundless!
    He laid all those riches aside,
That we might have riches eternal,
    And with Him forever abide.
                            —*Mrs. Frank A. Breck*

WHAT CHRISTMAS MEANS TO ME

Christmas to some means presents,
    To others a Christmas tree,
To some it may mean a party;
    That's not what it means to me.

To some it may mean a brand new dress,
    Or candy and cake and tea,
To some it may mean another good time;
    That's not what it means to me.

On Christmas we do receive presents,
  We have a Christmas tree, too,
But to me it means the Christ-Child's birth;
  Is that what it means to you?

—*Betty Smith*

COMFORT

What God Hath Promised

God hath not promised
    Skies always blue,
Flower-strewn pathways
    All our lives through;
God hath not promised
    Sun without rain,
Joy without sorrow,
    Peace without pain.

God hath not promised
    We shall not know
Toil and temptation,
    Trouble and woe;
He hath not told us
    We shall not bear
Many a burden,
    Many a care.

God hath not promised
    Smooth roads and wide,
Swift, easy travel,
    Needing no guide;
Never a mountain,
    Rocky and steep,
Never a river
    Turbid and deep.

But God HATH promised
    Strength for the day,
Rest for the labor,
    Light for the way,
Grace for the trials,
    Help from above,
Unfailing sympathy,
    Undying love.

—Annie Johnson Flint

Jesus Our Comforter

"As one whom his mother comforteth so will I comfort you."—Isaiah 66:13

When I'm blue and when I'm weary,
　　When all things on earth go wrong,
When my nights are long and dreary,
　　And my days have lost their song.

Then upon my knees I'm praying,
　　Then I feel Thee very near,
Then in sweet communion staying,
　　I can hear the answer clear.

Oh, how sweet is my devotion,
　　Oh, how sweet Thy presence feels;
Thou canst calm the mighty ocean,
　　Thou my wounded spirit heals.

Unto Thee all power is given,
　　On the land and on the sea,
Thou didst leave Thy home in Heaven,
　　Came to earth and died for me.

When my life down here is over,
　　When my race on earth is run,
When I'm sleeping 'neath the clover,
　　I'll hear Thy welcome words, "Well done."

In Heav'n I'll dwell in joy and gladness,
　　Seeing Jesus face to face,
In that home where comes no sadness,
　　I'll tell the story, "Saved by Grace."

'Tis indeed a wondrous story,
　　How He left His home above,
Giving up His heavenly glory
　　Saving us through His great love.

Now in gratitude let's give Him
　　All we are and hope to be,
Walking humbly in His footsteps,
　　Throughout all eternity.

—Clifford Lewis

"My Grace Is Sufficient For Thee"

"When, sin-stricken, burdened, and weary,
    From bondage I longed to be free,
There came to my heart the sweet message:
    'My grace is sufficient for thee.'

Though tempted and sadly discouraged,
    My soul to this refuge will flee,
And rest in the blessed assurance:
    'My grace is sufficient for thee.'

My bark may be tossed by the tempest
    That sweeps o'er the turbulent sea—
A rainbow illumines the darkness:
    'My grace is sufficient for thee.'

O Lord, I would press on with courage,
    Though rugged the pathway may be,
Sustained and upheld by the promise:
    'My grace is sufficient for thee.'

Soon, soon will the warfare be over,
    My Lord face to face I shall see,
And prove, as I dwell in His presence:
    'His grace was sufficient to me.'"

Passing Through

"When thou passest through the waters. . . . they shall not overflow thee. . .
Isa. 43:2

"When thou passest through the waters"—
    Deep the waves may be and cold,
But Jehovah is our refuge
    And His promise is our hold;
For the Lord Himself hath said it,
    He, the faithful God and true—
When thou comest to the waters
    Thou shalt not go down, but through.

Seas of sorrow, seas of trial,
    Bitterest anguish, fiercest pain,
Rolling surges of temptation
    Sweeping over heart and brain—
They shall never overflow us
    For we know His word is true;
All His waves and all His billows
    He will lead us safely through.

Threatening breakers of destruction,
    Doubt's insidious undertow,
Shall not sink us, shall not drag us
    Out to ocean depths of woe,
For His promise shall sustain us,
    Praise the Lord, whose word is true!
We shall not go down, or under,
    For He saith, "Thou passest through."

—Annie Johnson Flint

ARE YOU AT "WITS' END CORNER"?

"Are you standing at 'Wits' End Corner,'
    Christian, with troubled brow?
Are you thinking of what is before you,
    And all you are bearing now?
Does all the world seem against you,
    And you in the battle alone?
Remember—at 'Wits' End Corner'
    Is where God's power is shown.

Are you standing at 'Wits' End Corner,'
    Blinded with wearying pain,
Feeling you cannot endure it,
    You cannot bear the strain,
Bruised through the constant suffering
    Dizzy, and dazed, and numb?
Remember—at 'Wits' End Corner'
    Is where Jesus loves to come!

Are you standing at 'Wits' End Corner,'
    Your work before you spread,
Or lying, begun, unfinished
    And pressing on heart and head,
Longing for strength to do it,
    Stretching out trembling hands?
Remember—at 'Wits' End Corner'
    The Burden Bearer stands.

Are you standing at 'Wits' End Corner,'
    Yearning for those you love,
Longing and praying and watching,
    Pleading their cause above,
Trying to lead them to Jesus,
    Wond'ring if you've been true?
He whispers, at 'Wits' End Corner'
    'I'll win them as I won you.'

Are you standing at 'Wits' End Corner?'
    Then you're just in the very spot,
To learn the wondrous resources,
    Of Him who faileth not!
No doubt, to a brighter pathway
    Your footsteps will soon be moved,
But only at 'Wits' End Corner,'
    Is 'the God who is able,' proved."

THE STEPPING STONES

"Father, I fear! the night is dark, the river very wide;
I fear the slippery stepping-stones, the angry swirling tide."
"Courage, my child! give Me thy hand; heed not the water's roar,
I know each slippery stepping-stone, and I will guide thee o'er."

"Father, I fear the blinding rain! it makes me faint with fear;
I cannot see the stepping-stone, if it be far or near."
"Trust Me, my child, hold fast My hand, step where My steps
    have been;
The light shines in thy Father's home, though darkness
    intervene."

"Father, I fear the cruel hail, it smites me grievously,
Father, hold my trembling hand, I neither feel nor see!"
"My child, the Everlasting Arms are round thee all the way,
And fear and cold and pain shall pass, and night be turned to
      day."

—*M. H. S.*

My Every Day Need

"Grace when the sun is shining Lord,
  Grace when the sky is black,
  Grace when I get an unkind word,
  Grace on the too smooth track.

Grace when I'm elbowed into a nook,
  Grace when I get "my turn,"
  Grace when the dinner will not cook,
  Grace when the fire won't burn.

Grace when my duties all go wrong,
  Grace when they all seem right,
  Grace when I've gladness, praise and song,
  Grace when I have to fight.

Grace when my dress is fresh and new,
  Grace when it's frayed and old,
  Grace when my purse is empty too,
  Grace when it's full of gold.

Grace when the saved ones don't act saved,
  And throw the blame on me,
  Grace, when the grace I've asked and craved,
  Seems denied me, Lord, by Thee.

Grace when the midnight hours I tell,
  Grace when the morn is nigh,
  Grace when I'm healthy, strong and well,
  Grace should I come to die.

Lord grant Thy grace, till the gift I get,
  Up the steps of faith to climb,
  That the heart that seems inclined to fret,
  May keep smiling all the time.

Oh, Jesus, hear me and grant Thy grace,
My need to Thy Store I bring,
That, the proper one, in the proper place,
I may glorify THEE, MY KING!"

THE SAVIOR CAN SOLVE EVERY PROBLEM

The Savior can lift every burden,
    The heavy as well as the light;
His strength is made perfect in weakness,
    In Him there is power and might.

The Savior can bear every sorrow,
    In Him there is comfort and rest;
No matter how great the affliction,
    He only permits what is best.

The Savior can strengthen the weary,
    His grace is sufficient for all;
He knows every step of the pathway,
    And listens to hear when we call.

The Savior can break sin's dominion,
    The victory He won long ago;
In Him there is freedom from bondage,
    He's able to conquer the foe.

The Savior can satisfy fully
    The heart that the world cannot fill;
His presence will sanctify wholly
    The soul that is yielded and still.

The Savior can solve every problem,
    The tangles of life can undo;
There is nothing too hard for Jesus,
    There is nothing that He cannot do.
                                    —*Oswald J. Smith*

"It Is I, Be Not Afraid"

When the storm was fiercely raging
　　On the Lake of Galilee,
And their helpless bark was tossing
　　On the wild, tempestuous sea,
Walking on the raging waters
　　In a robe of Light arrayed,
Jesus came, oh, hear Him calling—
　　"It is I, be not afraid!"

When the storms of life are raging,
　　And the night is long and drear,
When our strength is spent with toiling,
　　And our spirit sinks with fear,
Oft again we see Him coming,
　　Swiftly hast'ning to our aid;
Often still we hear Him calling—
　　"It is I, be not afraid!"

When the night of death shall lower,
　　And the Jordan's surges roll,
When the hour and power of darkness
　　Overwhelm the sinking soul,
Then above the raging billows,
　　And night's deepest, darkest shade,
We shall hear Him calling to us—
　　"It is I, be not afraid!"

—A. B. Simpson

Thy Weakness — His Strength

"His grace is sufficient, whatever the pathway,
　　His strength in thy weakness shall perfected be;
So great is His love it never can weary
　　Of meeting thy need and of caring for thee.

His grace is sufficient, thou ne'er canst exhaust it,
　　Be strong in that grace which floweth to thee,
Draw largely, continually, out from His fulness,
　　He still is sufficient, He careth for thee.

Thou'rt nothing but weakness, His arms are around thee,
    Not a thing canst thou do, but simply lie still,
And learn in the pathway of simple dependence
    A song of thanksgiving, since this is God's will.

Then cling in thy weakness for He is beside thee,
    Upholding, supporting, sustaining thee still;
And know that the Father is only just working
    To mould thee and fashion thee unto His will.

Thy weakness He'll use to display His own glory,
    Resurrection strength then shall perfected be;
And thus thou shalt prove through the wilderness journey,
    His grace shall be always sufficient for thee."

HE WILL NEVER FAIL

Can the sun forget its rising?
    Can the stars forget to shine?
Can the moon forget its duty?
    Then can God His will resign.

Can the sea forget to roar?
    Can the waves cease and be still?
Can the waters stop giving?
    Then can God forget His will.

Can the skies above be measured?
    Can the foes of God prevail?
Can a man earth's structure fathom?
    Then God's promises can fail.

                    —*H. H. Savage*

LEAN HARD ON JESUS

Lean hard, sad heart, on Jesus, He knows thy secret grief,
And swift He is to succor, so swift to give relief;
Then let come cloud or sunshine, or skies be dull or clear,
Lean hard, sad heart, on Jesus, for thou hast nought to fear.

With Him 'tis ever sunshine, and clouds are far away,
With Him there is no darkness, but full meridian day;
Tho' winter's blast or summer's balm, or life or death should
    come,
Lean hard on Him, dear troubled heart, He's pledged to bring
    thee home.

Oh trust Him, heart! cast all thy care on Him who cares for you,
The clouds must break, at evening time, thou His clear light
    shall see;
The setting sun in richer beams shall make thy evening blest,
With all thy weight then lean on Him, and in His purpose rest.

Thou dost not see thy morning joys amidst thy evening fears,
Thou dost not see that morning songs result from evening tears;
'Tis when the darkness blackest hangs, like pall of deepest night,
That morning breaks, and ushers in, the longed-for orient light.

The dimness of those doubting eyes shall soon have passed away,
And fulness of divine surprise shall be your joy for aye,
And trials, crosses, sufferings past, now hard to understand,
Shall be explained, when darkness dies, in our Immanuel's land.
                        —*W. H. B.*

"I UNDERSTAND"
Psalm 50:15

Hast thou been hungry, child of mine?
I, too, have needed bread,
For forty days I tasted naught
Till by the angels fed;
Hast thou been thirsty? On the cross
I suffered thirst for thee;
I've promised to supply thy need,
My child, come unto me.

Perhaps thy way is weary oft,
Thy feet grow tired and lame,
I wearied when I reached the well,
I suffered just the same;
And when I bore the heavy cross
I fainted 'neath the load;
And so I've promised rest to all
Who walk the weary road.

Doth Satan sometimes buffet thee,
And tempt thy soul to sin?
Do faith and hope and love grow weak,
Are doubts and fears within?
Remember, I was tempted thrice
By this same foe of thine;
But he could not resist the Word,
Nor conquer power divine.

When thou art sad and tears fall fast
My heart goes out to thee,
For I wept o'er Jerusalem—
The place so dear to me;
And when I came to Lazarus' tomb
I wept—my heart was sore;
I'll comfort thee when thou dost weep,
Till sorrows all are o'er.

Do hearts prove false when thine is true?
I know the bitter dart,
I was betrayed by one I loved—
I died of broken heart;
I loved my own, they loved me not,
My heart was lonely too;
I'll never leave thee, child of mine,
My loving heart is true.

Art thou discouraged in thy work?
Doth ministry seem vain?
I ministered midst unbelief,
Midst those with greed of gain;
They would not hearken to my voice,
But scoffed with one accord;
Your labor never is in vain
If done unto the Lord.

Have courage, then, my faithful one,
I suffered all the way;
Thy sensitive and loving heart
I understand today;
Whate'er thy grief, whate'er thy care
Just bring it unto me;
Yea, in thy day of trouble, call,
I will deliver thee.

—*Sussane Umlauf*

THE LAST HYMN

"The sabbath day was ending
In a village by the sea,
The uttered benediction
Touched the people tenderly.

And they rose to face the sunlight
In the glowing lighted West,
And then hastened to their dwellings
For God's blessed boon of rest.

But they looked across the water
And a storm was raging there,
A fierce spirit moved about it
The wild spirit of the air.

It slashed the foaming billows
Till they thundered, groaned and boomed,
And alas, for any vessel
In that awful gulf entombed.

Very anxious were the people
On that rocky coast of Wales,
Lest the dawn of coming morrow
Should be telling awful tales,

When the sea had spent its passion
And should cast upon the shore,
Bits of wrecked and swollen victims,
As it oft had done before.

With the high winds blowing round her
A brave woman strained her eyes,
As she saw among the billows
A huge vessel fall and rise.

Oh, it did not need a prophet
To tell what the end must be,
For no ship could ride in safety
Near that shore on such a sea.

Then the pitying people hurried
From their homes and thronged the beach,
Oh, for power to cross the waters
And the perishing to reach.

Helpless hands were wrung in terror
Tender hearts grew cold with dread,
And the ship, urged by the tempest
On the fatal rock shore sped.

She has parted in the center
Oh, the half of her goes down,
God have mercy, in His Heaven
For to seek for those who drown!

Lo! when next the white shocked faces
Looked with terror on the sea,
Only one last clinging figure
On a spar was seen to be.

Nearer to the trembling waters
Came the wreck, tossed by the wave,
And the man still clung and floated
Though no power on earth could save.

Could we send him one short message?
Here's the trumpet, shout away,
'Twas the preacher's hand that took it,
And he wondered what to say.

Any memory of his sermon?
Firstly?—Secondly?—ah no,
There was but one thing to utter
In that awful hour of woe.

So he shouted through the trumpet
'Look to Jesus. Can you hear?'
And 'Aye, aye, sir,' rang the answer
O'er the waters loud and clear.

Then they listened, he was singing
'Jesus lover of my soul,'
And the winds brought back the echo
'While the nearer waters roll.'

Strange indeed it was to hear him—
'Till the storms of life be past,'
Singing bravely o'er the waters
'Oh, receive my soul at last.'

He could have no other refuge
'Hangs my helpless soul on Thee,'
'Leave, oh leave me not,' the singer
Dropped at last into the sea.

And the watchers looking homeward
Through their eyes by tears made dim,
Said, 'He passed to be with Jesus
With the singing of that hymn.' "

HE TAKES MY HAND

She's just a little kiddie
    Who walks by her mother's side,
And she'd rather go out walking
    Than to take a little ride.

She likes to skip and hop along,
    To run ahead and wait
For mother to catch up to her
    Down by the garden gate.

But sometimes when they go walking
    It gets hard for her to stand,
And when the road gets rocky,
    She says, "Mother, take my hand."

It's all right when paths are easy
    For her to skip along,
But when it's getting hard to walk
    She wants a hand so strong,

To reach down and take hold of hers
    To help her find the way,
"Mother, mother, hold my hand;"
    Is what you'll hear her say.

I guess that we're all children,
    Sometimes the way is bright,
Then we like to run along;
    But when the day grows night,

When the shadows lengthen,
    When the sky is overcast—
Or when we walk the valley
    When the day is done at last:

I think that we shall reach right up,
    I know He'll understand,
And we'll cry like weary children,
    "Lord Jesus, take my hand."

I know that He will reach right down
    To help us in our need,
For when we cannot help ourselves
    He'll always intercede.

Then when the journey's over
    And we stand on yonder strand,
Methinks that we shall ask again,
    "Lord Jesus, take my hand."
                —Louis Paul Lehman, Jr.

(Copyrighted by the author)

PEACE, PERFECT PEACE

Peace, perfect peace, in this dark world of sin?
The blood of Jesus whispers, peace within.

Peace, perfect peace, by thronging duties pressed?
To do the will of Jesus, this is rest.

Peace, perfect peace, with sorrows surging round?
On Jesus' bosom naught but calm is found.

Peace, perfect peace, with loved ones far away?
In Jesus' keeping we are safe, and they.

Peace, perfect peace, our future all unknown?
Jesus we know, and He is on the throne.

Peace, perfect peace, death shadowing us and ours?
Jesus has vanquished death and all its powers.

It is enough; earth's struggles soon shall cease,
And Jesus call us to heaven's perfect peace.
                                    —*Edward H. Bickersteth*

THE UNEXPECTED

I know not what may come today,
Some needy soul may cross my way;
Lord, give a word of cheer I pray,
    To meet the unexpected.

Perchance He may afresh reveal
Some wound that He alone can heal;
He understands, and He can deal
    With all the unexpected.

Perhaps some loss may come to me,
Some care, or some perplexity;
Then He my strength and stay shall be
    To face the unexpected.

How oft within the trivial round
So many trying things are found;
But He can make all grace abound
    For all the unexpected.

No matter what the call may be,
Or changes that may come to me;
His hand of love in all I see
    From sources unexpected.

Why should I ever have one fear,
Though oft the way be dark and drear?
For Christ my risen Lord draws near
    With blessings unexpected.
                                    —*F. Buckley*

THE WILD WHITE ROSE

It was peeping through the brambles, that little wild white rose,
Where the hawthorn hedge was planted, my garden to enclose;
All beyond was fern and heather, on the breezy, open moor;
All within was sun and shelter, and the wealth of beauty's shore.
But I did not heed the fragrance of flow'ret or of tree,
For my eyes were on that rosebud, and it grew too high for me.

In vain I strove to reach it through the tangled mass of green,
It only smiled and nodded behind its thorny screen.
Yet through that summer morning I lingered near the spot;
Oh, why do things seem sweeter if we possess them not?
My garden buds were blooming, but all that I could see
Was that little mocking wild rose hanging just too high for me.

So in life's wider garden there are buds of promise, too,
Beyond our reach to gather, but not beyond our view;
And like the little charmer that tempted me astray,
They steal out half the brightness of many a summer's day.
Oh, hearts that fail with longing for some forbidden tree,
Look up and learn a lesson from my white rose and me.

'Tis wiser far to number the blessings at my feet
Than ever to be sighing for just one bud more sweet.
My sunbeams and my shadows fall from a pierced hand,
I can surely trust His wisdom since His heart I understand;
And maybe in the morning, when His blessed face I see,
He will tell me why my white rose grew just too high for me.
                                            —*Ellen H. Willis*

'TIS SWEET TO TRUST HIM

My Lord is ever with me
    Along life's busy way;
I trust in Him completely
    For guidance day by day.

He's with me when I waken
    To start the day anew;
I whisper, "Lord, I love Thee;
    I pray Thee, keep me true."

He's with me through the morning
   To help me with my task;
My heart turns ever upward
   For peace and strength to ask.

All day I feel His presence;
   We have communion sweet;
He bids me bring my burdens
   And lay them at His feet.

When, kneeling at my bedside,
   My heart is full of praise,
I thank Him for His goodness
   And love that fill my days.

At night I am not fearful;
   I'm trusting in His care,
Secure, whatever happens,
   I know He still is there.

'Tis sweet to trust Him fully,
   And on His grace rely;
He gives me joy forever—
   A home beyond the sky!

—*Helen A. Lewis*

CONSECRATION

I Met the Master

"I had walked life's way with an easy tread,
Had followed where comforts and pleasures led,
Until one day in a quiet place
I met the Master face to face.

With station and rank and wealth for my goal,
Much thought for my body but none for my soul,
I had entered to win in life's mad race,
When I met the Master face to face.

I met Him and knew Him and blushed to see
That His eyes full of sorrow were fixed on me,
And I faltered and fell at His feet that day
While my castles melted and vanished away.

Melted and vanished, and in their place,
Naught else did I see but the Master's face;
And I cried aloud, 'Oh, make me meet
To follow the steps of Thy wounded feet.'

My thought is now for the souls of men;
I have lost my life to find it again,
E'er since one day in a quiet place
I met the Master face to face."

Obedience

I said: "Let me walk in the fields."
    He said: "No, walk in the town."
I said: "There are no flowers there."
    He said: "No flowers, but a crown."

I said: "But the skies are black;
    There is nothing but noise and din."
And He wept as He sent me back—
    "There is more," He said, "there is sin."

I said: "But the air is thick,
  And fogs are veiling the sun."
He answered: "Yet souls are sick,
  And souls in the dark undone!"

I said: "I shall miss the light,
  And friends will miss me, they say."
He answered: "Choose tonight
  If I am to miss you or they."

I pleaded for time to be given,
  He said: "Is it hard to decide?
It will not seem so hard in heaven
  To have followed the steps of your Guide."

I cast one look at the fields,
  Then set my face to the town;
He said, "My child, do you yield?
  Will you leave the flowers for the crown?"

Then into His hand went mine;
  And into my heart came He;
And I walk in a light divine,
  The path I had feared to see.

                              —*George MacDonald*

Is This Consecration?

"I'll go where you want me to go, dear Lord,
  Real service is what I desire;
I'll say what you want me to say, dear Lord—
  But don't ask me to sing in the choir.

I'll say what you want me to say, dear Lord,
  I like to see things come to pass;
But don't ask me to teach girls and boys, dear Lord—
  I'd rather just stay in my class.

I'll do what you want me to do, dear Lord,
  I yearn for the kingdom to thrive;
I'll give you my nickels and dimes, dear Lord—
  But please don't ask me to tithe.

I'll go where you want me to go, dear Lord,
    I'll say what you want me to say;
I'm busy just now with myself, dear Lord—
    I'll help you some other day."

SAVED, BUT—

"I am saved, but is self buried?
    Is my one, my only aim,
Just to honor Christ my Savior,
    Just to glorify His Name?

I am saved, but is my home life
    What the Lord would have it be?
Is it seen in every action,
    Jesus has control of me?

I am saved, but am I doing,
    Everything that I can do,
That the dying souls around me,
    May be brought to Jesus, too?

I am saved, but could I gladly,
    Lord, leave all and follow Thee;
If Thou callest can I answer,
    Here am I, send me, send me?"

MY HEART'S DESIRE

Cleanse my heart and fill me with Thy Spirit
    Satisfy the longings of my soul,
I crown Thee King and bid Thee hold the sceptre
    Yielding all, I'm now 'neath Thy control.
Have Thy way, for Thee alone—I'll follow;
    Too long I've followed self, rejecting Thee,
Now I lay my ALL upon the altar;
    Sanctify the gift and dwell with me.

All my plans and all of my ambitions,
　　All my dreams and all my earthly store,
Friends with all their ties that closely bind me
　　I ask Thee Lord to hold forever more.
Crucify the self that ruled within me;
　　I'll take the cross and gladly follow Thee;
Stamp Thy likeness on my heart forever,
　　Until Thy blessed image all shall see.

Stir my heart with love's intensest ardor
　　Teach me how to give, to serve, to pray;
Make my heart and life an unchoked channel
　　Of blessing to my fellow men each day.
Keep me humble, lowly and submissive,
　　Sweet in spirit, kind in thought and deed,
Until all who look see Jesus only
　　And precious souls to Thee, I then may lead!

—Helen G. Riggs

Speak Out for Jesus!

"You talk about your business,
　　Your bonds and stocks and gold;
And in all worldly matters
　　You are so brave and bold;
But why are you so silent
　　About salvation's plan?
Why don't you speak for Jesus,
　　And speak out like a man?

You talk about the weather,
　　And the crops of corn and wheat;
You speak of friends and neighbors
　　That pass along the street;
You call yourself a Christian,
　　And like the Gospel plan—
Then why not speak for Jesus,
　　And speak out like a man?

Are you ashamed of Jesus
    And the story of the cross,
That you lower His pure banner
    And let it suffer loss?
Have you forgot His suffering?
    Did He die for you in vain?
If not, then live and speak for Jesus,
    And speak out like a man.

I'd like to tell the story sweet
    Of Jesus. Wouldn't you?
To help some other folks to meet
    Their Savior. Wouldn't you?
I'd like to travel all the way .
    To where I'd hear my Jesus say:
'You've helped my work along today,'
    I'd like that. Wouldn't you?"

DOES IT PAY TO SERVE JEHOVAH?

Does it pay to serve Jehovah and reject the world's applause,
    Does it pay to serve Jehovah, though oppressed?
While the wicked seek their comfort in a rich and gilded hall,
    Does it pay to simply lean on Him and rest?

Does it pay to serve Jehovah and reject the world's applause,
    And receive instead its ridicule and jeers?
Does it pay to be subjected to false witness without cause?
    Does it pay to wait for heaven's future cheers?

Does it pay to take the Savior and refuse to take the world,
    Does it pay to think of worldly fame as loss?
Will it pay when all the glories of God's heaven are unfurled,
    To rejoice that we have stood beside the cross?

                                    —*H. H. Savage*

"Here Am I"

If Thou dost need a hand today,
    To clasp another hand on life's rough way
        Take mine, dear Lord, take mine.

If Thou art needing feet to tread
    In paths where sin to woe is wed,
        Use mine, dear Lord, use mine.

If Thou art needing lips today,
    For words that help and heal, to say,
        Fill mine, dear Lord, fill mine.

If Thou art needing eyes to see
    When souls begin to stray from Thee,
        Fit mine, dear Lord, fit mine.

But cleanse, dear Lord, and purify,
    And then each talent sanctify,
        Of mine, dear Lord, of mine.

                —*Mary E. Kendrew*

Life Worth Living

If all the wealth in all the world were mine,
And all the nations strove to do my will,
If I controlled the very stars that shine,
And could command the sun and wind, "Be still!"
But lacked the favor of Thy love divine,
It would be naught.

If I had perfect health and I could stay
Through countless ages strong and free from pain,
If all unpleasant things were swept away
And I had nothing else to do but reign,
I still would wish to turn to Thee and pray
As Thou hast taught.

Though I were blest with honor and with praise,
I could not find content from Thee apart,
I could not face the thought of endless days
To live without Thy love within my heart;
For how can I not walk along Thy ways,
Whom Thou hast bought?

                —*Beryl A. Wood*
             Southampton, England

LIVING BEFORE GOD

Just live thy life before thy Lord,
It matters not what others *say*,
Look thou upon HIS wondrous face,
And catch HIS smile from day to day.

Just live thy life before thy Lord,
It matters not what others *do*,
Thy actions will be weighed by Him,
Who metes out judgment just and true.

Just live thy life before thy Lord,
It matters not what others *think*,
Have conscience clear and step alert,
To follow Him and never shrink.

Just live thy life before thy Lord,
Rise to that higher, nobler plane,
With single eye HIS glory seek,
And thou shalt HIS approval gain.

Then on those lofty, sunlit heights,
The tempests far beneath may blow,
But not a breath can touch the soul,
Who lives that life while here below.

—*M. E. Rae*

NONE OF SELF AND ALL OF THEE

Oh, the bitter pain and sorrow
    That a time could ever be
When I proudly said to Jesus,—
    "All of self, and none of Thee."

Yet He found me; I beheld Him
    Bleeding on th' accursed tree;
And my wistful heart said, faintly,
    "Some of self, and some of Thee."

Day by day His tender mercy,
    Healing, helping, full and free,
Brought me lower, while I whispered,—
    "Less of self, and more of Thee!"

Higher than the highest heavens
  Deeper than the deepest sea,
"Lord, Thy love at last has conquered;
  NONE of self and ALL of Thee!"

  —Theodore Monod

THE OLD LAMP

"A lamp once hung in an ancient town
  At the corner of a street,
Where the wind was keen, and the way was dark,
  And the rain would often beat;
And all night long, its light would shine
  To guide the traveller's feet.

The lamp was rough and plain and old,
  And the storm had beaten it sore;
'Twas not a thing one would care to show,
  Whate'er it had been before,
But no one thought what the lantern was,
  'Twas the light that, within, it bore.

The lamp is a text for young and old,
  Who seek in a world of pride
To shine for their Lord and to show Him forth,
  And never their light to hide;
You are the lantern, a thing of naught,
  But Christ is the light inside."

A YIELDED LIFE

"All to Jesus now I give,
From this hour for Him to live;
While before His cross I bow,
He doth hear my humble vow.

Far as I at present know,
Every idol is laid low;
And, if ought remaineth still,
God shall even this reveal.

Oh! what peace now rules within!
Grace to triumph over sin;
Such as once I scarcely thought
Could in human heart be wrought.

Prostrate at Thy feet I fall,
Lord to Thee for help I call;
May I never more depart,
Love Thee with a constant heart.

Now my duty is to tell
Of this grace unspeakable;
Witnessing to all around
Full salvation I have found."

The Living Sermon

"I'd rather see a sermon than hear one any day,
I'd rather one would walk with me than merely tell the way;
The eye's a better pupil and more willing than the ear,
Fine counsel is confusing, but example's always clear;
The best of all the preachers are the men who live their creeds,
For to see good put in action is what everybody needs.

I soon can learn to do it, if you'll let me see it done,
I can watch your hands in action, your tongue too fast may run;
The lectures you deliver may be very wise and true,
But I'd rather get my lessons by observing what you do;
I may not understand the high advice you give,
But there's no misunderstanding how you act and how you live."

Will You Give It Up?

"I cannot give it up,
    The little world I know!
The innocent delights of youth,
    The things I cherish so;
'Tis true I love my Lord,
    And want to do His will,
And, oh, I may enjoy the world,
    And be a Christian still!

I love the hour of prayer,
　　I love the hymns of praise;
I love the blessed word that tells
　　Of God's redeeming grace,
But I am human still,
　　And while I dwell on earth,
God surely will not grudge the hours
　　I spend in harmless mirth!

These things belong to youth,
　　And are its natural right—
My pleasures, pastimes, and my friends,
　　The merry and the bright;
My Father's heart is kind;
　　He will not count it ill,
That my small corner of the world
　　Should please and hold me still!

And yet—'outside the camp,'
　　'Twas there my Savior died!
It was the world that cast Him forth,
　　And saw Him crucified;
Can I take part with those
　　Who nailed Him to the tree?
And where His name is never praised,
　　Is that the place for me?

Nay, world! I turn away,
　　Though thou seem fair and good;
That friendly outstretched hand of thine
　　Is stained with Jesus' blood;
If in thy least device
　　I stoop to take a part,
All unaware, thine influence steals
　　God's presence from my heart.

I miss my Savior's smile
　　Whene'er I walk thy ways;
Thy laughter drowns the Spirit's voice,
　　And chokes the springs of praise;
If e'er I turn aside
　　To join thee for an hour,
The face of Christ grows blurred and dim
　　And prayer has lost its power!

Farewell! Henceforth my place
    Is with the Lamb who died;
My Sovereign, while I have Thy love,
    What can I want beside?
Thyself, dear Lord, art now
    My free and loving choice,
In whom, though now I see Thee not,
    Believing, I rejoice.

Shame on me that I sought
    Another joy than this,
Or dreamt a heart at rest with Thee
    Could crave for earthly bliss!
These vain and worthless things,
    I put them all aside;
His goodness fills my longing soul,
    And I am satisfied.

Lord Jesus, let me dwell
    Outside the camp with Thee!
Since Thou art there, then there alone
    Is peace and home for me;
Thy dear reproach to bear
    I'll count my highest gain,
Till Thou return, my banished King,
    To take Thy power and reign."

JESUS ONLY

Once it was the blessing,
    Now it is the Lord;
Once it was the feeling,
    Now it is His Word;
Once His gifts I wanted,
    Now Himself alone;
Once I sought for healing,
    Now the Healer own.

Once 'twas painful trying,
   Now 'tis perfect trust;
Once a half salvation,
   Now the uttermost;
Once 'twas ceaseless holding,
   Now He holds me fast;
Once 'twas constant drifting,
   Now my anchor's cast.

Once 'twas busy planning,
   Now 'tis trustful prayer;
Once 'twas anxious caring,
   Now He has the care;
Once 'twas what I wanted,
   Now what Jesus says;
Once 'twas constant asking,
   Now 'tis ceaseless praise.

Once it was my working,
   His it hence shall be;
Once I tried to use Him,
   Now He uses me;
Once the power I wanted,
   Now the mighty One;
Once for self I labored,
   Now for Him alone.

Once I hoped in Jesus,
   Now I know He's mine;
Once my lamps were dying,
   Now they brightly shine;
Once for death I waited,
   Now His coming hail,
And my hopes are anchored,
   Safe within the veil.

                —A. B. Simpson

BE STILL

Be still, my soul and listen,
For God would speak to thee,
And while the tempest's raging
Thy refuge He would be.

Be still, and cease to struggle,
Seek not to understand;
The flames will not destroy thee,
Thou'rt in the Father's hand.

And when the burden's heavy,
He seeks to make thee pure,
To give thee faith and patience
And courage to endure.

The way is not too hard for thee,
Endure the chastening rod;
Thy gold shall only be refined,
Be still, submit to God.

—*G. W. S.*

KEPT FOR JESUS

Oh, to be "kept for Jesus!"
Kept by the power of God;
Kept from the world unspotted,
Treading where Jesus trod.

Oh, to be "kept for Jesus!"
Serving as He shall choose;
"Kept" for the Master's pleasure,
"Kept" for the Master's use.

Oh, to be "kept for Jesus!"
Kept from the world apart;
Lowly in mind and spirit,
Gentle and pure in heart.

Oh, to be "kept for Jesus!"
Oh, to be all His own!
Kept to be His forever,
Kept to be His alone!

Oh, to be "kept for Jesus!"
Lord at Thy feet I fall;
I would be "nothing, nothing,"
Thou shalt be "all in all."
—*Edith E. Cherry*

WOULD I? WOULD YOU?

"One day in loved Jerusalem,
There rushed a shrieking, maddened crowd,
Upon a lowly kneeling form,
Before his God and Savior bowed;
And when with cruel stones they crushed
His beautiful and gentle life,
He prayed the Father to forgive
Their ignorance and raging strife;
This man was Stephen, Lo, a Jew,
Who died for Christ,
Would I? Would you?

See! far upon a lonely isle,
An aged man with snowy locks,
Exiled to labor in the mines,
His only temple wind-swept rocks;
Ah! once he leaned on Jesus' breast,
And gazed with fond adoring eyes
Into that face where love divine
Still beams upon us from the skies;
This man was John, beloved, a Jew,
Witness for Christ,
Am I? Are you?

A Galilean fisher stood
Amid a fierce and angry throng;
No tremor spoke of hidden fear;
His face was peaceful, calm and strong,
And when they nailed him to a cross,
As they had nailed his blessed Lord,
He gloried thus to die for Christ,
And counted it a rich reward,
This man was Peter, Lo, a Jew,
Who died for Christ,
Would I? Would you?

A captive bound was brought one day
To Nero's judgment seat at Rome;
For Christ he wore the heavy chain,
For Christ he had no wealth nor home;
The noblest martyr Rome could boast
Of all the thousands that she slew,
The great apostle, sent by God
To Gentiles with the message true;
This man was Paul, e'en Paul the Jew,
Who died for Christ,
Would I?   Would you?"

NOTHING BETWEEN

Nothing between my soul and the Savior,
   Naught of this world's delusive dreams;
I have renounced all sinful pleasure,
   Jesus is mine; there's nothing between.

Nothing between, like worldly pleasure,
   Habits of life though harmless they seem
Must not my heart from Him ever sever,
   He is my all; there's nothing between.

Nothing between, like pride or station,
   Self or friends shall not intervene,
Though it may cost me much tribulation,
   I am resolved; there's nothing between.

Nothing between, e'en many hard trials,
   Though the whole world against me convene;
Watching with prayer and much self denial,
   I'll triumph at last with nothing between.

Nothing between my soul and the Savior,
   So that His blessed face may be seen;
Nothing preventing the least of His favor,
   Keep the way clear! Let nothing between!

               —*C. A. Tindley*

DETERMINATION

It Couldn't Be Done

Somebody said that it couldn't be done
    But he with a chuckle replied,
That "maybe it couldn't," but he would be one
    Who wouldn't say so till he'd tried;
So he buckled right in with a trace of a grin
    On his face. If he worried, he hid it.
He started to sing as he tackled the thing
    That couldn't be done, and he did it!

Somebody scoffed, "Oh, you'll never do that;
    At least no one ever has done it;"
But he took off his coat and he took off his hat
    And the first thing we knew he'd begun it.
With a lift of his chin and a bit of a grin,
    Without any doubting or quiddit,
He started to sing as he tackled the thing
    That couldn't be done, and he did it!

There are thousands to tell you it cannot be done,
    There are thousands to prophesy failure;
There are thousands to point out to you one by one,
    The dangers that wait to assail you;
But just buckle in with a bit of a grin
    Just take off your coat and go to it;
Just start in to sing as you tackle the thing
    That "cannot be done," and you'll do it!

—Edgar A. Guest

(From *The Path to Home*, Copyrighted by the Reilly & Lee Co., Chicago.
Used by permission.)

Don't Quit

"When things go wrong, as they sometimes will,
When the road you're trudging seems all up hill,
When the funds are low and the debts are high,
And you want to smile, and you have to sigh,
When care is pressing you down a bit,
Rest if you must, but don't you quit!

Life is queer with its twists and turns,
As every one of us sometimes learns,
And many a failure turns about,
When he might have won had he stuck it out;
Don't give up, though the pace seems slow,
You may succeed with another blow.

Often the goal is nearer than
It seems to a faint and faltering man,
Often the struggler has given up,
When he might have captured the Victor's cup;
And he learned too late, when the night slipped down,
How close he was to the golden crown.

Success is failure turned inside out,
The silver tint of the clouds of doubt,
And you can never tell how close you are,
It may be near when it seems afar;
So stick to the fight when you're hardest hit,
It's when things seem worse that you mustn't quit."

I WILL!

There are doors forever closed against
    The weak and timid one,
There are mountain peaks he cannot climb,
    There are tasks he'll ne'er get done;
But all things wait for him who smiles,
    As steady he pulls the hill,
Though others say it can't be done,
    His answer is, "I Will!"

There are throngs to take the broad highway
    That winds 'neath shady trees,
The world is full of jostling crowds,
    Seeking ways of ease;
But where the way is steep and rough
    And getting rougher still,
There walk a few determined souls
    Who dare to say, "I Will!"

The one who quails and says, "I Can't,"
    Will never win the day,
The prize ne'er goes to him who quits,
    Or falters in the way;
The truly brave are those who keep
    A faith that fears no ill,
There's room above the sordid crowd
        For him who says, "I Will!"

                            —*W. Brandt Hughes*

TRUE TO CHRIST I'LL BE

True to Christ I'll be
    Through all eternity,
He's my Savior, He's my guide,
    He is always by my side;

I love Him more each day,
    I'll serve Him all the way;
Yes, true to Christ I'll always be
    Through all eternity.

                            —*Clifford Lewis*

GIVE US MEN

"Give us men to match our mountains,
Give us men to match our plains,
Men with empires in their purpose
Men with throbbing, conquering brains.

Give us men to lead our nation,
Give us men with holy zeal,
Men aflame with truth and vision
Men who bear the heavenly seal.

Give us men who love the Bible,
And it's precepts do obey,
Give us men who have convictions
And are Christians all the way.

Give us men who follow Jesus
Give us men who love their Lord,
Men with hearts pure and courageous
Men led by God's Eternal Word."

"Keep Pegging Away"

"Men seldom mount at a single bound
 To the ladder's very top;
They must slowly climb it, round by round,
 With many a start and stop;
And the winner is sure to be the man
 Who labors day by day,
For the world has learned that the safest plan
 Is to just keep pegging away.

You have read, of course, about the hare
 And the tortoise—the tale is old,
How they ran a race—it counts not where
 And the tortoise won, we are told;
The hare was sure he had time to pause
 And to brouse around and play,
So the tortoise won the race because
 He just kept pegging away.

A little toil and a little rest
 And a little more earned than spent,
Is sure to bring to an honest heart
 A blessing of glad content;
And so—though skies may frown and smile—
 Be diligent day by day;
Reward shall greet you after while
 If you just keep pegging away."

The Dreamer

Back of the beating hammer
 By which the steel is wrought,
Back of the workshops clamor
 The seeker may find a thought;
The thought that is ever master
 Of iron or steam or steel,
Which rises above disasters
 And tramples them under heel.

The drudge may fret or tinker
　　Or labor with lusty blows,
But back of him stands the thinker
　　The clear-eyed man who knows;
For into each plow and saber
　　Each piece and part and whole,
Must go the brains of labor
　　Which gives the work a soul.

Back of the motors humming
　　Back of the bells that ring,
Back of the hammers drumming
　　Back of the cranes that swing;
There is an eye which scans them
　　Watching through stress and strain,
There is the mind which plans them
　　Back of the brawn—the brain.

Might of the roaring boiler
　　Force of the engines thrust,
Strength of the sweating toiler
　　Greatly in these we trust;
But back of them stands the thinker
　　The schemer, who drives things through,
But back of the job stands the dreamer
　　Who is making his dreams come true.

　　　　　　　　　　　—Burton Brailey

GET SOMEWHERE!

Are you groping for a blessing,
　　Never getting there?
Listen to a word in season,
　　Get somewhere!

Are you struggling for salvation
　　By your anxious prayer?
Stop your struggling, simply trust, and—
　　Get somewhere!

Are you worn and heavy laden,
　　Pressed with many a care?
Cast your burden on the Lord, and—
　　Get somewhere!

Would you know the Great Physician
    Who your sickness bare?
Simply take Him at His word, and—
    Get somewhere!

Does the answer seem to linger
    To your earnest prayer?
Turn your praying into praise, and—
    Get somewhere!

Are you looking for your mission,
    What to do and dare?
Cease your dreaming, start at something—
    Get somewhere!

You will never know His fulness
    Till you boldly dare
To commit your all to Him, and—
    Get somewhere!

All your efforts are but building
    Castles in the air,
Till you answer yes to God, and—
    Get somewhere!

—*A. B. Simpson*

YOUTH IS ON THE MARCH!

"Remember now thy Creator in the days of thy youth, while the evil days come not, nor the years draw nigh when thou shalt say, I have no pleasure in them."—Ecclesiastes 12:1

Youth is on the march!
    On every hand we see
Many flags unfurled,
    Calling you and me.

Youth is on the march!
    They're tramping to and fro;
Many paths to tread,
    Be careful where you go.

Youth is on the march!
    Can't you hear their cry?
A loyal group are they,
    Willing to live or die.

Youth is on the march!
   And sad will be the day
If through his haunts of sin,
   The devil leads the way.

Youth is on the march!
   Blindly down they go
To a place of sin and shame,
   Of agony and woe.

Some are marching with the Lord
   Towards the pearly gate,
Where we'll live for evermore,
   There our loved ones wait.

Why not fall in line today,
   Don't you want to go?
It pays to do His blessed will,
   We'll reap just what we sow.

We will march the streets of gold
   In that city bright,
Free from darkness, pain, or death,
   Where Jesus is the light.

—Clifford Lewis

THE SCOUT WHO STICKS

"You may talk of your Scouts who are strong on the hike,
Who are there on the trail, in the woods and the like;
You may have all the signalers, eagles, and stars,
First aiders, athletes, and sea-scouting tars;
But if from all Scouts you will give me my pick,
I'll fasten my choice on the Scout who will stick.

There's a job to be done, it's a tough one, I fear;
It may take a week, it may take a year,
Who's going to do it? Here comes the chap,
He takes off his coat, he throws down his cap,
Looks at the job, shuts his jaws with a click—
Fellows, that's him, the Scout who will stick.

Problems arise as the job goes along,
Nothing works right and everything's wrong;
When things look the blackest some Scouts will say—
'Oh, yes, what's the use?' and then beat it away;
But someone fights on through the thin and the thick,
And we find at the end the Scout who will stick."

RESULTS AND ROSES

"The man who wants a garden fair,
Or small or very big,
With flowers growing here and there,
Must bend his back and dig.

The things are mighty few on earth
That wishes can attain;
Whate'er we want of any worth
We've got to work to gain.

It matters not what goal you seek;
Its secret here reposes;
You've got to dig from week to week
To get results or roses."

"IF"

(With Apologies to Rudyard Kipling)

IF YOU CAN keep "the faith" when those about you
    Are losing it and seeking something new;
IF YOU CAN stand the firmer though they flout you
    As being simple and old fashioned, too;
IF YOU CAN put your hand in Christ's, and feeling
    The marks of Calvary's scars upon your palm,
Can gladly say "Amen" to all His dealing,
    Or change the sigh into a joyous psalm.

IF YOU CAN laugh when human hopes are banished,
    When castles fall and cherished prospects die;
And just keep on, though earthly props have vanished,
    Content to see the pattern by and by;
IF YOU CAN meet abuse without complaining,
    And greet your unkind critic with a smile,
If, conscious that your human love is waning,
    You claim a Calvary love that knows no guile;

IF YOU CAN bear the unjust imputation
    Without a murmur or revengeful thought,
And even forfeit rights and reputation,
    Because HIS glory is the one thing sought;
IF YOU CAN give an honest commendation
    To him whose work looms larger than your own,
Or scorn to speak the word of condemnation
    To him who falls or reaps what he has sown.

IF YOU CAN give consent to Calvary's dying,
    And live again in resurrection power,
IF YOU CAN claim the victory, not by trying,
    But RESTING in His triumph every hour;
IF YOU CAN be content with His provision,
    Though others seem to prosper and succeed;
Nor let repining mar the heavenly vision,
    And simply trust in God for every need.

IF YOU CAN let the mind of Christ possess you,
    To think on "things of good report" and true;
And ever let the love of Christ obsess you,
    Constraining everything you say and do;
IF YOU CAN find in Him your highest treasure,
    Let HIM hold sway o'er heart and soul and limb,
Then LIFE is yours, and blessing without measure,
    And—what is more—YOU'LL LIVE AND REIGN WITH HIM!
                                        —*Reginald Wallis*

"I can . . . . through Christ."—Phil. 4:13

ON TO THE GOAL

"On to the goal! Press on!
    Alone, yet unafraid;
He cut the path who beckons thee,
    On then, and undismayed.

On to the goal! Press on!
    The Eyes that are a flame
Are watching thee, what then are men
    What matter praise or blame?

On to the goal! Press on!
  Look not behind thee now,
When just ahead lies His 'Well done,'
  And crowns await thy brow.

On to the goal! Press on!
  Blind, deaf, and sometimes dumb,
Along the uphill, blood-marked road,
  Hard after Christ, press on!"

EASTER

"Why Weepest Thou?"

O dry your tears, ye sons of men;
    The Lord's not dead, but risen!
The mighty stone is rolled away
    From death's cold, gloomy prison.

In clouds transplendent with the light,
    Angelic hosts attended,
Triumphant over all His foes,
    The Lord, our God, ascended.

If He were still in Joseph's tomb,
    We might hang harps on willows,
And bid farewell to every hope
    Before the surging billows.

We might spend all our strength in tears,
    And break our hearts with sorrow,
And see no ray of light ahead,
    No happy, bright tomorrow.

But, oh, why do you weep today?
    What means this sad behavior?
If you, like Mary, dry your tears,
    You'll see a living Savior!

List, how He calls you by your name!
    Behold, the empty prison!
Run! send the tidings to all men—
    The Lord, the Lord is risen!

—*J. F. M.*

REJOICE!

Rejoice, ye Christians, everywhere!
From that dark tomb so sad
Christ is risen; He's not there!
Rejoice and be ye glad!

The Easter message we would give
To all for whom He died;
Trust Him today and you will live
Forever at His side!

This glorious message we'll proclaim
To each and every nation,
Till all have heard His precious name
And of His great salvation!

—*Clifford Lewis*

EASTER

"Sing, soul of mine, this day of days,
The Lord is risen.
Toward the sunrising set thy face,
The Lord is risen.
Behold, He giveth strength and grace;
For darkness, light; for morning, praise;
For sin, His holiness; for conflict, peace.

Arise, O soul, this Easter Day!
Forget the tomb of yesterday
For thou from bondage art set free;
Thou sharest in His victory
And life eternal is for thee
Because the Lord is risen!"

FAITH

GOD'S BANK AIN'T BUSTED YET!

The bank had closed; my earthly store had vanished from my
        hand;
I felt that there was no sadder one than I in all the land.
My washerwoman, too, had lost her little mite with mine,
And she was singing as she hung the clothes upon the line.
"How can you be so gay?" I asked; "Your loss don't you regret?"
"Yes, ma'm, but what's the use to fret? God's bank ain't busted
        yet!"

I felt my burden lighter grow; her faith I seemed to share;
In prayer I went to God's great throne and laid my troubles there.
The sun burst from behind the clouds, in golden splendor set;
I thank God for her simple words: "God's bank ain't busted yet!"

And now I draw rich dividends, more than my hands can hold
Of faith and love and hope and trust and peace of mind untold.
I thank the Giver of it all, but still I can't forget
My washerwoman's simple words: "God's bank ain't busted yet!"

Oh, weary ones upon life's road, when everything seems drear,
And losses loom on every hand, and skies seem not to clear;
Throw back your shoulders, lift your head, and cease to chafe
        and fret.
Your dividend will be declared: "God's bank ain't busted yet!"
        —*Alice P. Moss*

CAN'T WE TRUST HIM?

The God who made the flowers,
    And the God who made the sea,
Will not this loving Father
    Watch over you and me?

The Creator of the planets,
    Who made the sun to shine,
Surely He is mindful
    Of both your needs and mine.

Lord, give us faith to trust Thee
    And never doubt again;
Thou art the same forever
    From beginning to the end.

We would be ever mindful
    Of Thy rich bounties sweet;
Grant that we'll ne'er forsake Thee
    Until in Heav'n we meet.

There in that home eternal—
    Beside the golden shore,
We'll thank Thee, praise, and love Thee
    Forever and evermore.

Up there beyond life's sorrows
    The saints of God will meet,
Where we shall know no sadness,
    Our loved ones we shall greet.

There with the Lord and the angels,
    We'll know no pain nor tears,
But only peace and happiness
    Throughout the endless years.

Now that we have the vision
    Of joy and promised rest,
For Christ our blest Redeemer
    Let's always do our best.

—Clifford Lewis

FAITH

"Faith—substance of things hoped for,
    Evidence of that unseen,"
Faith—moving, conquering energy;
    Faith—patient and serene:
Faith bridges chasms where the mind
    Breaks down in utter loss;
Faith lifts the load and moves ahead,
    When we bow beneath the cross.

Faith moves into the realm of God,
  And there in perfect peace,
We find the great reality—
  Our earthly strivings cease—
That which is unseen is greater
  Than that which we now behold,
The riches of eternity
  Outweigh all earthly gold.

Faith knows what reason never grasps,
  Faith is our light and sight,
The pulsing of the vital heart,
  The star in darkest night:
Faith is the basis of our life,
  The grounds of our salvation,
Not "Do and live!" but "Believe and live!"
  Is God's great proclamation.

                    —*Louis Paul Lehman, Jr.*
              (Copyrighted by the author)

FAITH THAT WORKS

"Faith is needed all the way,
  Faith to toil and faith to pray,
  Faith to learn and faith to teach,
  Faith to practice, faith to preach;
  Faith to start each day anew,
  Faith to do our duty, too;
  Faith to help the weak along,
  Faith to bear, in patience, wrong;
  Faith to smile, though sad within,
  Faith to conquer every sin,
  Faith to ask Him for His care
  While we earthly trials bear;
  Faith to smother every sigh,
  Faith to live and faith to die."

LORD, INCREASE MY FAITH

"O for a faith that will not shrink
Though pressed by many a foe,
That will not tremble on the brink
Of poverty or woe.

That will not murmur nor complain
Beneath the chastening rod,
But in the hour of grief or pain
Can lean upon its God.

A faith that shines more bright and clear
When tempests rage without,
That when in danger knows no fear,
In darkness feels no doubt.

Lord, give me such a faith as this
And then, whate'er may come,
I taste e'en now the hallowed bliss
Of an eternal home."

TRUST

"When nothing whereon to lean remains,
When strongholds crumble to dust;
When nothing is sure but that God still reigns,
That is just the time to trust.

'Tis better to walk by faith than sight,
In this path of yours and mine;
And the pitch-black night, when there's no other light,
Is the time for our faith to shine."

FATHER

A Toast to Father

"Just be a pal to us, fathers,
    Share in our troubles and joy,
Give your advice when we need it
    And remember, you once were a boy.

Perhaps we do things that are trying
    And things that are apt to annoy,
But don't be too hard on us, fathers,
    Remember, you once were a boy.

We'd like to go fishing when you do,
    There's nothing we more would enjoy,
Than to angle the stream with you, dad,
    Just as you did as a boy.

If sometimes we earn a chastising
    And you may deem the rod to employ,
Lay it on—but this we're advising,
    Just think back when you were a boy.

And now, as I close, I'm reflecting
    On the size of the debt that we owe,
To father for aid and directing
    And showing the way we should go.

Unhappy the son who has failed in his part
    As a comrade, a pal, and a friend,
To his father who holds him so dear to his heart
    With a guardianship without end.

And unhappy the father who never has won
    The comfort, the solace, the joy,
That comes from the kinship of father and son
    And the love and respect of his boy.

But happy the father, and happy the son
    Whose lives in true unison blend,
Who each in the other has confidence won
    As father, as son, and as friend.

But just one word more, oh father, I pray
 Lest our confidence you should destroy,
Just try to look back and retrace the old track
 And remember when you were a boy."

To Any Daddy

"There are little eyes upon you, and they're watching night and
  day;
There are little ears that quickly take in every word you say;
There are little hands all eager to do everything you do;
And a little boy who's dreaming of the day he'll be like you.

You're the little fellow's idol; you're the wisest of the wise,
In his little mind about you, no suspicions ever rise;
He believes in you devoutly, holds that all you say and do,
He will say and do, in your way when he's grown up like you.

There's a wide-eyed little fellow, who believes you're always
  right;
And his ears are always open, and he watches day and night;
You are setting an example every day, in all you do,
For the little boy who's waiting to grow up to be like you."

Understanding

"When I was young and frivolous and never stopped to think,
When I was always doing wrong, or just upon the brink;
When I was just a lad of seven and eight and nine and ten,
It seemed to me that every day I got in trouble then;
And strangers used to shake their heads and say I was no good,
But father always stuck to me—it seems he understood.

I used to have to go to him 'most every night and say
The dreadful things that I had done to worry folks that day.
I know I didn't mean to be a turmoil round the place,
And with the womenfolks about forever in disgrace;
To do the way they said I should, I tried the best I could,
But though they scolded me a lot—my father understood.

He never seemed to think it queer that I should risk my bones,
Or fight with other boys at times, or pelt a cat with stones;
An' when I'd break a window pane, it used to make him sad,
But though the neighbors said I was, he never thought me bad;
He never whipped me, as they used to say to me he should;
That boys can't always do what's right—it seemed he understood.

Now there's that little chap of mine, just full of life and fun,
Comes up to me with solemn face to tell the bad he's done;
It's natural for any boy to be a rougish elf,
He hasn't time to stop and think and figure for himself,
And though the womenfolks insist that I should take a hand,
They've never been a boy themselves, and they don't understand.

Some day I've got to go up there, and make a sad report
And tell the Father of us all where I have fallen short;
And there will be a lot of wrong I never meant to do,
A lot of smudges on my sheet that He will have to view.
And little chance for heavenly bliss, up there, will I command,
Unless the Father smiles and says: 'My boy, I understand.'"

WATCH YOUR STEP!

"Father, there's a call for you—
    Watch your step!
Little eyes see all you do—
    Watch your step!
Little feet go daddy's way,
    Follow you from day to day,
Lead, oh lead them not astray—
    Watch your step!

Your example is their guide—
    Watch your step!
'Daddy does,' they say with pride,
    Watch your step!
Children may do as you say—
    'As you do,' 'twill be some day—
Watch your step!

Boys aspire to be like you
    Watch your step!
Is your path safe to pursue?
    Watch your step!
If some day they stain your name—
    And on you should place the blame,
Oh, how you will blush with shame—
    Watch your step!

Walk the safe and narrow way;
    Watch your step!
Let the children hear you pray—
    Watch your step!
Would you ways of wisdom teach
    With God's truth their young hearts reach?
Watch your step!

Father, near your journey's end,
    Watch your step!
Let the Savior be your Friend,
    Watch your step!
He will guide your feet aright,
    To the land of pure delight—
Would you walk with Him in white?
    Watch your step!"

FRIENDSHIP

God Bless You!

"I seek in prayerful words, dear friend,
My heart's true wish to send you;
That you may know that, far or near,
My loving thoughts attend you.

I cannot find a truer word,
Nor fonder to caress you;
Nor song nor poem I have heard
Is sweeter than 'God bless you.'

God bless you! So I've wished you all
Of brightness life possesses;
For can there any joy at all
Be thine, unless God blesses?

God bless you! So I breathe a charm
Lest grief's dark night oppress you;
For how can sorrow bring you harm
If 'tis God's way to bless you!"

Just One Friend

"If life gives only one true friend,
One who is faithful to the end,
Then Life has given more than gold
The greatest joy a heart can hold.

If just one friend is ours to share
To understand, believe, and care,
Then life is sweet, complete and true
Because of just one friend like you."

IF YOU HAVE A FRIEND WORTH LOVING

"If you have a friend worth loving,
Love him—yes, and let him know
That you love him, ere life's evening
Tinge his brow with sunset glow.
Why should good words ne'er be said
Of a friend—till he is dead?

If you hear a song that thrills you,
Sung by any child of song,
Praise it—do not let the singer
Wait deserved praises long.
Why should one who thrills your heart
Lack the joy you may impart?

If a silvery laugh goes rippling
Through the sunshine on his face,
Share it—'tis the wise man's saying
For both grief and joy a place.
There's health and goodness in the mirth
In which an honest laugh has birth.

If your work is made more easy
By a friendly, helping hand,
Say so—speak out brave and truly
Ere the darkness veils the land.
Should a brother workman dear
Falter for a word of cheer?

Scatter thus your seeds of kindness,
All enriching as you go,
Leave them—trust the Harvest-Giver;
He will make each seed to grow.
So, until the happy end,
Your life shall never lack a friend."

A Friend Like You

In appreciation of their daily prayers and kind encouragement,
I dedicate this poem to all my friends.

It's great to have a friend like you,
    Along life's weary road,
One who is always kind and true,
    To help me bear my load.

It's great to have a friend like you,
    While trav'ling here below,
One who tries to help me through
    As Heaven-ward I go.

It's great to have a friend like you,
    As I journey through this life;
I thank you now for all you do
    To banish doubt and strife.

I'd like to have more friends like you,
    True-blue until the end;
And if my wish comes ever true,
    I must be such a friend.

                           —Clifford Lewis

True Friendship

"The world goes on from year to year,
With many a friend to make it dear,
With many a smile and many a song
To speed the golden days along;

But most of all, my thanks are due,
For having one such friend as you!"

A HEAVENLY FRIEND

A loving friend is Jesus,
    Kind-hearted, loyal, and true—
A friend who is always near us
    To help and bring us through.

A loving friend is Jesus,
    A comforter and guide—
One who will never leave us
    Who is walking by our side.

A loving friend is Jesus,
    Our salvation He has bought,
He hears our supplications,
    Helps us to live as we ought.

A loving friend is Jesus,
    Though often our love is weak,
He understands and pardons
    When we forgiveness seek.

A loving friend is Jesus,
    He's faithful to the end,
And by consistent living
    His cause we can defend.

A loving friend is Jesus,
    For, one day, we shall dwell
With Him and with the angels,
    If with our soul 'tis well.

—Paul Tucker
Bath, England

GUIDANCE

The Lord's Leading

"Strangely" has He led thee, strangely,
  By a long and lonesome way,
Sometimes where the sunbeams lingered,
  Sometimes where the shadows lay?

Have thy feet grown often weary,
  And the tears bedimmed thine eyes,
When thy path grew steep and rugged,
  Nought above but leaden skies?

Hast thou been perplexed and troubled,
  When the thunder roared o'erhead,
Sorely wondering midst the darkness
  Where thy feet were meant to tread?

Hast thou wondered why He led thee
  By such strange and lonesome ways,
Why thy future lay enshrouded
  In a dark, mysterious haze?

Wondered why thy feet are guided,
  Where the shadows thickly lie,
Why the storms and why the darkness,
  Why that cold and cloudy sky?

Hush! He speaks, He whispers to thee:
  "By a way thou hast not known,
I have led thee by a pathway
  Marked out solely for Mine own."

Faithless child, He fain would teach thee,
  What a God of love thou hast,
Guiding all thy steps with wisdom,
  Leading safely home at last!

Soon thou'lt learn the "why" and "wherefore,"
  Although now thou canst not know
Why the storm and cloud are sent thee,
  Just because He loves thee so.

—M. E. Rae

THE RED SEA PLACE IN YOUR LIFE

Have you come to the Red Sea place in your life,
    Where, in spite of all you can do,
There is no way out, there is no way back,
    There is no other way but—through?
Then wait on the Lord with a trust serene,
    Till the night of your fear is gone,
He will send the wind, He will heap the floods,
    He says to your soul, "Go on!"

And His hand will lead you through—clear through—
    Ere the watery walls roll down,
No foe can reach you, no wave can touch,
    No mightiest sea can drown;
The tossing billows may rear their crests,
    Their foam at your feet may break,
But over their bed you may walk dry shod,
    In a path that your Lord will make.

In the morning watch, 'neath the lifted cloud,
    You shall see but the Lord alone,
Where He leads you on from the place by the sea,
    To the land that you have not known;
And your fears shall pass as your foes have passed,
    You shall be no more afraid;
You shall sing His praise in a better place,
    A place that His hand has made.

                                    —*Annie Johnson Flint*

(Copyright by Evangelical Publishers, Toronto, Canada)

THE MASTERPIECE

With eager hands I took life's turning loom
And sought to make my life a shining one,
Then with the shuttle of desire and greed
I wove the colors of a dying sun.

Into my masterpiece I blended there
The nuance of a newly-wakened dawn;
Asking not for succor, aid, nor guide,
In my own earthly strength I labored on.

From off the skein I chose gold threads, nor knew
That darker threads make golden tints more bright;
Nor did I deem that roses bloom more fair
When washed in dewy tears of sable night.

But one day as I wove—my earth-bound hands
In burdened weariness fell from the loom;
My eyes were dazzled with the tinsel shine
And longed for darker shades of twilight gloom.

With streaming eyes I gazed into the blue
To seek God's potent wisdom from above;
'Twas then He took my hand within His own
And gazed on me with wondrous eyes of love.

My weariness dropped from me like a cloak,
Unstilled desires found a calm surcease;
Now with His hand on mine, I let Him weave
My life into a shining Masterpiece.

Then when the shuttle is forever stilled,
And when the worn out loom of life has spun
Its one last thread into my tapestry—
God will gaze on my work and say "Well done!"
                              —*Betty Perpetuo*

CHOOSE THOU FOR ME

I dare not choose my lot,
    I would not if I might,
Choose Thou for me, my God,
    So shall I walk aright.

The kingdom that I seek
    Is Thine; so let the way
That leads to it be Thine,
    Else surely I might stray.

Take Thou my cup, and it
    With joy or sorrow fill,
As best to Thee may seem,
    Choose Thou my good and ill.

Choose Thou for me my friends,
  My sickness or my health,
Choose Thou my cares for me,
  My poverty or wealth.

Not mine—not mine the choice,
  In things both great and small,
Be Thou my Guide, my Strength,
  My Wisdom and my All.

—*H. Bonar*

The Tapestry

Somehow we learn to piece the threads again
Into some semblance of a pattern! Colors run
.To riot, never brave enough for rain,
Or burned and bleached and faded from the sun
Must be replaced by others that are strong.
Somehow we know—if we are wise—before too long
To choose the dark threads cheerfully and to leave
For other days, the brighter bits of gold—
Learn through the years, but slowly, not to grieve
When threads are torn from off the piece we hold.

Somehow we learn, if faith be never lost,
To weave, though blind to wisdom, all the colors in,
Sparing no thought of scarlet that has cost
More than the courage we could give—the thin,
Grey bits of monotone—the black of fear—
We learn from God's own teaching not to stand too near
Where colors are distorted to our gaze—
We wait His time, when with the weaving past
Forgetting the strange contour of our days
Within the many patterns of His love, at last
The colors blend together and we see
One glorious pattern for His tapestry.

—*Ruth Margaret Gibbs*

CHASTENING

"Now no chastening for the present seemeth to be joyous, but grievous: nevertheless afterward it yieldeth the peaceable fruit of righteousness unto them which are exercised thereby."—Heb. 12:11

"I know not why His hand is laid
    In chastening on my life,
Nor why it is my little world
    Is filled so full of strife.

I know not why, when faith looks up
    And seeks for rest from pain,
That o'er my sky fresh clouds arise
    And drench my path with rain.

I know not why my prayer so long
    By Him has been denied,
Nor why, while others' ships sail on,
    Mine should in port abide.

But I do know that God is Love,
    That He my burden shares,
And though I may not understand,
    I know for me He cares.

I know the heights for which I long
    Are often reached through pain,
I know the sheaves must need be threshed
    To yield the golden grain.

I know that, though He may remove
    The friends on whom I lean,
'Tis that I thus may learn to love
    And trust the One unseen.

And, when at last I see His face
    And know as I am known,
I will not care how rough the road
    That led me to my Home."

TRUST IN THE MASTER WEAVER

"When dark gray threads are woven
    And seem so out of line,
Trust in the Master Weaver,
    Who planned the whole design.

In all life's choicest patterns,
    Dark threads are always there
To make the gay threads brighter,
    The gold and rose more fair.

At times, it all seems intricate
    And hard to understand,
But trust in the Master Weaver
    And His steady, guiding hand."

BUT GOD—

I know not, but God knows;
    Oh, blessed rest from fear!
All my unfolding days
    To Him are plain and clear.
Each anxious, puzzled "Why?"
    From doubt or dread that grows,
Finds answer in this thought:
    I know not, but He knows.

I cannot, but God can;
    Oh, balm for all my care!
The burden that I drop
    His hand will lift and bear,
Though eagle pinions tire,—
    I walk where once I ran,—
This is my strength, to know
    I cannot, but God can.

I see not, but God sees;
  Oh, all-sufficient light!
My dark and hidden way
  To Him is always bright;
My strained and peering eyes
  May close in restful ease,
And I in peace may sleep;
  I see not, but He sees.

—Annie Johnson Flint

(Copyright by Evangelical Publishers, Toronto, Canada)

HE KEEPS THE KEY

"Is there some problem in your life to solve,
Some passage seeming full of mystery?
God knows, who brings the hidden things to light.
  He keeps the key.

Is there some door closed by the Father's hand
Which widely opened you had hoped to see?
Trust God and wait—for when He shuts the door
  He keeps the key.

Is there some earnest prayer unanswered yet,
Or answered not as you had thought 'twould be?
God will make clear His purpose by-and-by.
  He keeps the key.

Have patience with your God, your patient God,
All wise, all knowing, no long tarrier He,
And of the door of all thy future life
  He keeps the key.

Unfailing comfort, sweet and blessed rest,
To know of EVERY door He keeps the key
That He at last when just He sees 'tis best,
  Will give it thee."

HEAVEN

In Heaven

"There will be no unemployment
In that land beyond the sky;
There will be no wage reduction
In that sweet, sweet bye and bye.

There will be no breadlines forming
On that morning bright and fair;
When the saints of earth are gathered
To a better home up there.

There will be no big depressions
For there'll be no greed for gain;
Every soul will have a blessing
Every heart be freed from pain.

There will be no strikes or lockouts
Earthquakes, warfare, sin or shame;
For we'll gather with our Savior
Singing glory to His Name."

It Is Better Farther On

"Hark! a voice from Eden stealing,
Such as but to angels known,
Hope its song of cheer is singing
'It is better farther on.'

Hope is singing, still is singing,
Softly in an undertone,
Singing as if God had taught it,
'It is better farther on.'

Night and day it sings the same song,
Sings it when I sit alone;
Sings it so the heart may hear it,
'It is better farther on.'

On the grave it sits and sings it,
  Sings it when the heart would groan,
Sings it when the shadows darken,
  'It is better farther on.'

Farther on! O how much farther?
Count the mile-stones one by one;
No! not counting, only trusting,
'It is better farther on'."

Looking Ahead

"And God shall wipe away all tears from their eyes; and there shall be no more death, neither sorrow, nor crying, neither shall there be any more pain; for the former things are passed away."—Revelation 21:4

This old life is filled with sorrows,
  Filled with heartaches, pains and fears;
Here we have our disappointments,
  Cheeks are lined with bitter tears;

But our Father, God in Heaven,
  Longs to help us overcome,
Then when this short life is ended,
  He will take us safely home.

Yes, our lives may be all gloomy,
  Clouds may shadow every day,
But we'll understand it better
  When the mists are rolled away.

When the Savior comes to take us
  To that land of rest up there,
We'll forget the disappointments
  Which were here so hard to bear.

So let's think of God and Heaven,
  Let's look up and laugh and smile,
And forget our disappointments—
  We'll be leaving in a while—

For that home to be with Jesus,
  For that home, so bright and fair,
For that land that's filled with gladness,
  And we'll find no sorrows there.

                              —*Marvin Lewis*

WE'LL SEE THEM AGAIN

The sun has gone to rest beneath the lake,
    And one by one the little stars awake;
But do not think because it slips from view,
    The sun has bid the earth a last adieu.
We say the sun has "gone to rest" when night
    Drops a veil that dims the mortal sight;
But it has risen on another world,
    The petals of its golden bloom unfurled,
And there the robin in the treetop sings,
And warmth and light awake all waiting things.

And so "at rest" is what we sometimes say
    Of that dear one who gently slipped away;
But he has simply vanished from the earth
    To find elsewhere a new and glorious birth;
Lost to our sight a little tearful while,
    His tender voice, his quick and eager smile.
But surely as the faithful, rising sun
    Returns to bless our eyes, so will this one
Be waiting when the dawn of dawns appears,
    So put away your sorrow and your tears,
And know that you will see him face to face,
Whose light already shines in that far place.
                    —Lois Parrish

WHEN THE STARS PASS AWAY

"The stars look up to God,
    The stars look down on me,
The stars shine over the earth,
    The stars shine over the sea.

The stars may shine a million years,
    A million years and a day,
But Christ and I shall live and love,
    When the stars have passed away."

INFLUENCE

You Can Never Tell

"You never can tell when you send a word
    Like an arrow shot from the bow,
By an archer blind, be he cool or kind
    Just where it will chance to go.

It may pierce the heart of your dearest friend
    Tipped with its poison or balm;
To a stranger's heart, in life's great mart
    May carry its pain or its calm.

You never can tell when you do an act
    Just what the result will be,
For with every deed, you are sowing a seed
    Tho' its harvest you may never see.

Each kindly act is an acorn dropped
    In God's productive soil,
Tho' you may not know, yet the trees will grow
    And shelter the brows that toil.

You never can tell what your thought will do
    And bring you hate or love,
For thoughts are things, and their eerie wings
    Go swifter than a carrier dove.

They follow the law of the universe
    Each thing must create its kind,
And often as not in truth to bring back
    The things that went out of your mind."

Someone Is Following You

Don't forget that day by day
Someone is following you;
Be careful what you say,
Be careful what you do.

Don't forget as you go along
Someone is following you;
Watch to avoid the wrong,
Watch the path you pursue.

God help you this truth to see:
Someone is following you;
Be strong! His witness be,
Be strong! Live always true.

—Clifford Lewis

EXAMPLE

"'Twas a sheep, not a lamb, that strayed away,
  In the parable Jesus told—
A grown-up sheep that had gone astray
  From the ninety and nine in the fold.

Out on the hillside, out in the cold,
  'Twas a sheep the Good Shepherd sought;
And back to the flock, safe into the fold,
  'Twas a sheep the Good Shepherd brought.

And why for the sheep should we earnestly long
  And as earnestly hope and pray?
Because there is danger; if they go wrong,
  They will lead the lambs astray.

For the lambs will follow the sheep, you know,
  Wherever the sheep may stray;
When the sheep go wrong, it will not be long
  Till the lambs are as wrong as they.

And so with the sheep we earnestly plead,
  For the sake of the lambs, today;
If the sheep are lost, what terrible cost
  Some lambs will have to pay!"

JOY

SMILE

"The thing that goes the farthest
    Towards making life worth while,
Which costs the least and counts the most,
    Is just a pleasant smile.
The smile that bubbles from a heart
    That loves its fellow men,
Will drive away the clouds of gloom
    And coax the sun again.
It is full of worth, and goodness too,
    With manly kindness blent;
It is worth a million dollars
    And it doesn't cost a cent.

There is no room for sadness
    When we see a cheery smile,
It always has the same good looks,
    It's never out of style.
It nerves us on to try again
    When failure makes us blue,
The dimples of encouragement
    Are good for me and you.
It pays a higher interest
    For it is merely lent;
It is worth a million dollars
    And doesn't cost a cent.

A smile comes very easy,
    You can wrinkle up with cheer
A hundred times before you
    Can squeeze out a soggy tear.
It ripples out moreover
    To the heart-strings that will tug,
And always leaves an echo
    That is very like a hug;
So smile away, folks understand
    What by a smile is meant;
It is worth a million dollars
    And doesn't cost a cent."

KEEP SWEET

There's a little secret
    Worth its weight in gold,
Easy to remember,
    Easy to be told;
Changing into blessing
    Every curse we meet,
Turning hell to heaven,
    This is all—keep sweet.

Make us kind and gentle,
    Harmless as the dove;
Giving good for evil,
    Meeting hate with love;
What though trials press us,
    What though tempests beat,
Naught can move or harm us
    If we just keep sweet.

Storms may rage around us,
    Waves may sweep the deck,
But with hatches covered
    Naught our bark can wreck;
Sorrow cannot crush us,
    Satan must retreat
If within our spirit
    All is right and sweet.

Sweet when things are bitter,
    Sweet when hearts are sad;
Giving songs for sighing,
    Making others glad;
In the quiet household,
    On the bustling street,
Everywhere and always,
    Jesus, keep us sweet.

When our foes assail us,
  When our friends betray,
When our brightest prospects
  Wither and decay,
Christ can fill our sadness
  With a joy replete,
Turning grief to gladness,
  Making sorrow sweet.

Fountain in the desert,
  Song amid the night,
Beacon in the darkness,
  Star of hope and light;
Sunshine mid the tempest,
  Shadow from the heat—
Like the Blessed Master,
  Make us, keep us, sweet.

—*A. B. Simpson*

JOYOUS SERVICE

It's grand to love the Savior
  And read His Holy Word;
I thank Him for the quick'ning life
  Within my heart He stirred.

It's grand to love the Savior
  And to commune with Him;
He says, "Win others to me,
  Don't let your light grow dim."

It's great to love the Savior,
  Won't you accept Him too?
He'll satisfy your longings
  And bring rich joys to you.

It's grand to love the Savior,
  While in this world I stay,
And know His gracious promise
  To come for me some day.

—*Paul Tucker*
Bath, England

My Secret

Shall I tell you what it is that keeps me singing,
    Never minding whether it be shade or shine?
'Tis because His own glad song is singing in me,
    'Tis because the Saviour's joy is always mine.

Shall I tell you what it is that keeps me springing,
    With a strength that smiles at sickness and decay?
'Tis because the Life of Jesus fills my being,
    And the Living Bread sustains me day by day.

Shall I tell you why my foes no longer vex me,
    And my cares and fears and doubtings all are o'er?
'Tis because I've given my burdens all to Jesus,
    And He leads me forth in triumph evermore.

Shall I tell you why my life is now so easy?
    'Tis because this wretched self has ceased to be;
Once it caused me all my troubles, but it's buried,
    And it is no longer I, but Christ in me.

Shall I tell you why I love to work for Jesus?
    'Tis because His blessed Spirit works in me;
I have but to let Him use me, His the power,
    Mine the recompense to share, the fruit to see.

Shall I tell you why I love to tell of Jesus?
    'Tis because there's nothing else so good and true;
There's no other name or story worth the telling,
    Without Jesus what could helpless sinners do?

Shall I tell you why I'm watching for His coming?
    'Tis because of all my future He's the sum;
This will be my joy forever—Jesus only—
    And I long, and look, and pray for Him to come.

                           —*A. B. Simpson*

MOTHER

MOTHERS

I walk into my garden fair,
And see the flowers blooming there;
I nestle in a shady nook
And listen to the babbling brook;
I seem to hear the lowing herds,
The honey bees, the song of birds;

In my dreams I onward go
To watch the sunset's golden glow;
I look into the sky at night
And see the stars shining bright;
And in the distance covering all
I see the shadow moonbeams fall;

I stand beside the ocean blue
And think of all that's good and true;
Of all the lovely things God made
There's one above all others—
He took the best from all of these
And made them into "Mothers."

—*Laura V. Cline*

MOTHERHOOD

"If I could write with diamond pen,
    Use ink of flowing gold,
The love I have for my mother dear
    Could then not half be told.

Her sympathy has been my stay,
    Her love my guiding light,
Her gentle hand hath soothed my ills;
    She's ever guided right.

A precious friend has mother been,
    Stood by me all the way,
No sacrifice has been too great;
    Such love one can't repay.

So wonderful has mother been,
   So gentle, kind and good,
That I have learned to reverence
   That sweet word, 'Motherhood.' "

MY MOTHER'S NAME

"No painter's brush or poet's pen,
   In justice to her fame,
Has ever reached half high enough
   To write my mother's name.

Make ink of tears and golden gems
   And sunbeams mixed together,
With holy hand and golden pen,
   Go write the name of Mother.

In every humble tenant house,
   In every cottage home,
In marble courts and gilded halls
   And on every palace dome:

On mountains high, in valleys low,
   In every land and clime,
On every throbbing human heart,
   That blessed name enshrine.

Take childhood's light and manhood's age,
   Celestial canvass given,
In beauty trace her name and face
   And go hang it up in heaven.

Thrice upward to the Heavenly Home,
   And midst music soft and sweet,
Thank Jesus for your Mother's name,
   And write it at His feet."

BEAUTIFUL HANDS

"Such beautiful, beautiful hands!
    They are neither white nor small,
And you, I know, would scarcely think
    That they were fair at all;
I've looked on hands whose form and hue
    A sculptor's dream might be,
Yet are these aged, wrinkled hands
    More beautiful to me.

Such beautiful, beautiful hands!
    Though heart were weary and sad,
Those patient hands kept toiling on,
    That children might be glad;
I almost weep, as I look back
    To childhood's distant day,
I think how those hands rested not
    When mine were at their play.

Such beautiful, beautiful hands!
    They're growing feeble now,
For time and pain have left their mark
    On hand, and heart, and brow;
Alas, alas, the weary time,
    And the sad, sad day to me,
When 'neath the daisies out of sight,
    Those hands will folded be.

But oh, beyond this shadowy damp,
    Where all is bright and fair,
I know full well those dear old hands
    Will palms of victory bear;
Where crystal streams thro' endless years
    Flow over golden sands,
And when the old grow young again
    I'll clasp my Mother's hands."

AT MY MOTHER'S KNEE

"I have worshipped in churches and chapels,
　　I've prayed in the busy street,
I have sought my God and have found Him
　　Where the waves of the ocean beat,
I have knelt in the silent forest,
　　In the shade of some ancient tree,
But the dearest of all my altars,
　　Was raised at my mother's knee.

I have listened to God in His temple,
　　I've caught His voice in the crowd,
I have heard Him speak when the breakers
　　Were booming long and loud;
Where the winds play soft in the tree tops
　　My Father has talked to me,
But I never have heard Him clearer
　　Than I did at my mother's knee.

God make me the man of her vision
　　And purge me of selfishness!
God keep me true to her standards
　　And help me to live to bless!
God hallow the holy impress
　　Of the days that used to be,
And keep me a pilgrim forever
　　To the shrine at my mother's knee."

MY MOTHER'S PRAYERS

"Among the treasured pictures
　　That I've hung on memory's wall,
There's one that's clearer than the rest
　　And sweeter far than all:
'Tis a picture of my mother
　　When I, a little chap,
Was folded in her loving arms,
　　To slumber on her lap;
I felt her hands caress my head,
　　I heard her softly say,
'Dear Jesus, take this little life
　　And use it every day.'

There must have been a mighty weight
    Behind that simple prayer,
For through the seasons, year on year,
    The picture lingers there,
And whether I'm on hill or plain
    Or on the deep blue sea,
The memory of that sacred scene
    Forever comforts me;
Among the treasured pictures
    That I've hung on memory's wall,
My mother's supplication
    Is the sweetest one of all."

ARE ALL THE CHILDREN IN?

"I think oftimes as the night draws nigh,
    Of an old house on the hill,
Of a yard all wide, and blossom-starred,
    Where the children played at will.

And when the night at last came down,
    Hushing the merry din,
Mother would look all around and ask,
    'Are all the children in?'

'Tis many and many a year since then,
    And the old house on the hill,
No longer echoes to childish feet,
    And the yard is still, so still.

But I see it all as the shadows creep,
    And though many the years have been
Since then I can hear my mother ask,
    'Are all the children in?'

I wonder if, when the shadows fall,
    On the last short earthly day,
When we say goodbye to the world outside
    All tired with our childish play,

When we meet the Lover of boys and girls,
    Who died to save them from sin,
Will we hear Him ask as mother did,
    'Are all the children in?' "

THE NAME OF JESUS

The Power of Jesus' Name
Phil. 2:9, 10; Mark 16:17, 18

My only hope, my only plea
    The Blood of Jesus shed for me,
His righteousness, my only claim
    I come, dear Lord, in Jesus Name.

We know that Name which Thou hast given
    Above all names in earth or Heaven,
That at that Name each knee shall bow
    And all, His Lordship shall allow.

And as we thus present His Name
    Before Thy Throne—our only claim—
All sin and sorrow must subside
    As thus we in our Savior hide.

In Christ we more than conquerors are
    In battles near and battles far,
For Satan is a conquered foe
    Through Him whose mighty Name we know.

Lift up the standard of His Name!
    Put all the hosts of Hell to shame!
Let not His Banner suffer loss
    Who won our Victory on the Cross!

—M. E. H.

Glory to the Name of Jesus!

Glory to the Name of Jesus!
    Once it stood for sin and shame;
Now the songs of earth and heaven
    Join to bless that glorious Name.

Pardon through the Name of Jesus!
    Free from guilt, and fault, and blame,
We may stand beloved, accepted
    As we come in Jesus' Name.

Victory through the Name of Jesus!
    Once for us He overcame,
And we conquer sin and Satan
    Only in our Captain's Name.

Power through the Name of Jesus!
    All His power our faith may claim,
God will work His wonders through us
    When we use that mighty Name.

Healing in the Name of Jesus!
    How it thrills our suffering frame,
When we learn to take from Jesus
    Life and healing in His Name.

Tell abroad the Name of Jesus;
    'Round the world His love proclaim
Till earth's saved and ransomed millions
    Join to praise the Savior's Name.

                      —A. B. Simpson

WITHIN THE NAME OF JESUS

Within the Name of Jesus
    Where peace and plenty lie,
I rest, securely sheltered—
    No evil can come nigh.

Within the Name of Jesus
    From condemnation free,
He cancelled each and every sin
    That I might ransomed be.

Within the Name of Jesus
    His power and might are mine,
And Satan is a conquered foe
    By that great Power Divine.

Within the Name of Jesus
    Sheltered from every storm,
The Hiding Place of all who trust—
    From every false alarm.

Within the Name of Jesus
    All upward shall ascend,
To greet Him at His Coming
    With joys that never end.

                      —M. E. H.

BLESSED BE HIS NAME

"I have a Friend, whose faithful love
    Is more than all the world to me,
'Tis higher than the heights above,
    And deeper than the boundless sea;
So old, so new, so strong, so true,
Before the earth received its frame,
HE LOVED ME—Blessed be His name!

He held the highest place above,
    Adored by all the sons of flame,
Yet, such His self-denying love,
    He laid aside His crown and came
To seek the lost, and at the cost
Of heavenly rank and earthly fame,
HE SOUGHT ME—Blessed be His name!

It was a lonely path He trod,
    From every human soul apart,
Known only to Himself and God
    Was all the grief that filled His heart;
Yet from the track, he turned not back
'Till, where I lay in want and shame,
HE FOUND ME—Blessed be His name!

Then dawned at last that day of dread
    When, desolate, yet undismayed,
With wearied frame and thorn-crowned head
    He, now forsaken and betrayed,
Went up for me—to Calvary,
And, dying there in grief and shame,
HE SAVED ME—Blessed be His name!

Long as I live, my song shall tell
    The wonders of His matchless love;
And, when at last I rise to dwell
    In the bright home prepared above,
My joy shall be His face to see,
And, bowing then with loud acclaim,
I'LL PRAISE HIM—Blessed be His name!"

NEW YEAR

Facing a New Year

"I know not what awaiteth me
As dawns another year,
The path untrod I can not see
Yet knows my heart no fear.

Though dark the path may be, or light
A smooth or rugged way,
I ever shall be led aright
While I for guidance pray.

I know not whether short or long
My pilgrimage may be,
I'll daily praise my Lord in song
For all His love to me.

And as the years shall onward roll
And day by day be mine,
I'll seek to lead some precious soul,
To Christ, the way divine.

My God shall be my strength and stay
While sojourning here below,
He will supply my need alway
His Word assures me so.

With joy I greet the opening year
It cannot bring me ill,
Since Christ, my Lord is ever near,
My soul with peace to fill."

Prayer for the New Year

"What shall I ask for the coming year?
What shall my watchword be?
What wouldst Thou do for me, dear Lord?
What can I do for Thee?

Lord, I would ask for a year of love,
    That I may love Thee best;
Give me the love that faileth not,
    Beneath the hardest test.

Lord, I would ask a year of prayer,
    Teach me to walk with Thee;
Breathe in my heart Thy Spirit's breath;
    Pray Thou Thy prayer in me.

Lord, I would ask for the dying world,
    Stretch forth Thy mighty hand;
Thy truth proclaim, Thy power display,
    In this and every land."

THE OLD YEAR AND THE NEW

Into the Silent Places
    The Old Year goes tonight,
Bearing old pain, old sadness,
    Old care, and old delight,
Mistakes and fears and failures,
    The things that could not last—
But naught that e'er was truly ours
    Goes with him to the past.

Out of the Silent Places
    The Young Year comes tonight,
Bringing new pain, new sadness,
    New care and new delight;
Go forth to meet him bravely,
    The New Year all untried,
The things the Old Year left with us—
    Faith, Hope, and Love—abide.

                    —*Annie Johnson Flint*

The New Leaf

"He came to my desk with quivering lip;
The lesson was done.
'Have you a new leaf for me, dear Teacher?
I have spoiled this one!'
I took his leaf, all soiled and blotted,
And gave him a new one, all unspotted,
Then into his tired heart I smiled:
'Do better now, my child.'

I went to the throne with trembling heart;
The year was done.
'Have you a new year for me, dear Master?
I have spoiled this one!'
He took my year, all soiled and blotted,
And gave me a new one, all unspotted,
Then into my tired heart He smiled:
'Do better now, my child!' "

New Year

In the happy coming year
    Not one sin is written down;
    Not a sorrow, not a frown.
Shall I make its record clear?

Will the year my pathway bless?
    What if pain should be my part?
    What if sorrow wring my heart?
Could I bear life's bitterness?

God is at the helm for me;
    All is well if He shall guide,
    He will let no ill betide;
From all fear my heart is free.

'Tis a shining, glad New Year;
    Not one wrong is written down;
    Tho' it bring me cross or crown,
Let me make its record clear!

—Mrs. Frank A. Breck

ANOTHER YEAR

"Another year is dawning!
    Dear Master, let it be
In working, or in waiting,
    Another year with Thee.

Another year of mercies,
    Of faithfulness and grace,
Another year of gladness,
    In the shining of Thy face.

Another year of service,
    Of witness to Thy love,
Another year of training
    For holier work above.

Another year is dawning,
    Dear Master, let it be
On earth, or else in heaven,
    Another year with Thee!"

NEW YEAR'S PRAYER

May this New Year's greatest blessing
    Be the fulness of the Lord,
Drawing you to sweet communion
    With Himself—in full accord.

May His Word be your foundation
    For each thought and purpose true,
That His Holy Spirit's working
    May work out God's will in you.

                                    —M. E. H.

God's Will

"I asked the New Year for some motto sweet,
Some rule of life by which to guide my feet,
I asked and paused; it answered soft and low,
    'God's will to KNOW.'

Will knowledge then suffice? New Year, I cried,
But ere the question into silence died
The answer came, 'No, this remember too,
    God's will to DO.'

Once more I asked, is there still more to tell?
And once again the answer sweetly fell;
'Yes, this one thing all other things above,
    God's will to LOVE'."

Unafraid

My presence shall go with thee,
    Beloved child of Mine!
Then why shouldst thou be fearful,
    Or why shouldst thou repine?
No danger can o'ertake thee
    When I am at thy side—
My presence shall go with thee,
    And I will be thy guide!

My presence shall go with thee!
    Though heavy be thy load,
Though dark may be the midnight,
    Though rough may be the road,
In sunshine and in shadow
    Commit thine all to Me—
My presence shall go with thee,
    And I will care for thee!

—*E. Margaret Clarkson*

PRAYER

The Secret

I met God in the morning,
When my day was at its best;
And His presence came like sunrise
With a glory in my breast.

All day long the Presence lingered,
All day long He stayed with me;
And we sailed in perfect calmness
O'er a very troubled sea.

Other ships were blown and battered,
Other ships were sore distressed,
But the winds that seemed to drive them,
Brought to us both peace and rest.

Then I thought of other mornings,
With a keen remorse of mind,
When I, too, had loosed the moorings,
With the Presence left behind.

So I think I know the secret,
Learned from many a troubled way;
You must seek Him in the morning,
If you want Him through the day.
—Ralph Cushman

The Christian's Daily Dozen

"First, turn your heart to God for grace,
Before you look on any face.

Next, breathe a word of thankful greeting
To Him who watched while you were sleeping.

Now, if you find this hard to do,
Invoke your will to help you through.

Just clinch your hand or turn your head,
'Twill drive the night mists from your bed.

Next, say a verse or hum an air
To make an atmosphere of prayer.

At length, when mind is keenly turning,
Repeat some new verse you are learning.

Then it will surely clear your vision
To voice in words the day's decision;

To talk with Christ about your work,
For Heaven can never bless a shirk.

And do not make another motion,
Until you kneel in sweet devotion.

And now, prepared the day to meet,
Arise and stand upon your feet.

Then, from the table while you're dressing,
Glean something from the Book of Blessing;

So go you forth with smile to greet
The first and every heart you meet.

And all day long your soul will thrive,
And men will thank God you're alive."

AFLAME FOR GOD

From prayer that asks that I may be
Sheltered from winds that beat on Thee,
From fearing when I should aspire,
From faltering when I should climb higher,
From silken self, O Captain, free
Thy soldier who would follow Thee.

From subtle love of softening things,
From easy choices, weakenings,
Not thus are spirits fortified,
Not this way went the Crucified;
From all that dims Thy Calvary,
O Lamb of God, deliver me.

Give me the love that leads the way,
The faith that nothing can dismay,
The hope no disappointments tire,
The passion that would burn like fire,
Let me not sink to be a clod:
Make me Thy fuel, Flame of God.

—*Amy Carmichael*

TEACH ME TO PRAY

"I often say my prayers
But do I always pray?
Or do the wishes of my heart
Go with the words I say?

I may as well kneel down
And worship gods of stone,
As offer to the living God
A prayer of words alone.

For words without the heart
The Lord will never hear,
Nor will He to that child attend
Whose prayers are not sincere.

Lord, show me what I need
And teach me how to pray,
And help me when I seek Thy grace
To mean the words I say."

LIVE THE WAY YOU PRAY

"I knelt to pray when day was done
And prayed, 'O Lord bless every one,
Lift from each saddened heart the pain,
And let the sick be well again.'

And then I woke another day
And carelessly went on my way,
The whole day long I did not try
To wipe a tear from any eye.

I did not try to share the load
Of any brother on my road,
I did not even go to see
The sick man just next door to me.

Yet once again when day was done
I prayed, 'O Lord bless every one.'
But as I prayed, into my ear
There came a voice that whispered clear:

'Pause hypocrite, before you pray,
Whom have you tried to bless today?
God's sweetest blessings always go
By hands that serve Him here below.'

And then I hid my face and cried,
'Forgive me, God, for I have lied,
Let me but live another day
And I will live the way I pray.' "

CREATE IN ME A CLEAN HEART

O Thou who walketh on the wings of wind
    Blow bare the secrets of my inmost heart,
And clear away unconscious sins I've sinned
    As well as conscious ones that wound and smart;
Make it a little sanctuary where
Thou wilt restore Thy chastened child in prayer.

Then like a wind-harp tune it up to praise
    So all its seasons shall like spring-time be,
As when peach blossoms on the soft warm days
    Drift down pink petals and sweet odors free,
Or when fresh water-springs gush close to hand
By paths that otherwise were arid sand.
                   —Grace W. Haight

GOD FIRST

In my bedroom hangs this motto,
    And its place is near the door,
So that it may e'er remind me,
    God all else must be before!

Never do I cross the threshold,
    But the motto seems to say—
"Just a word with God, thy Father,
    Ere thou goest on thy way."

When I'm dressing in the morning,
    As I see it hanging there,
It reminds me of my duties,
    Help for which I seek in prayer.

Duties, burdens, worries, troubles,
    All may come to me this day,
How can I prepare to meet them?
    How, I ask, except I pray?

When I plan fresh undertakings,
    Then the motto seems to say,
"Don't in thy own strength begin it,
    First of all, about it pray!"

When I'm ready dressed for walking,
    Perhaps with little time to spare;
Still I cannot leave my bedroom,
    When I see the motto there—

Till I kneel for just a moment,
    And in earnest, secret prayer,
Place myself and all my goings
    In my Heavenly Father's care.

Nightly, too, the motto speaketh,
   When for rest I would prepare,
Then it whispers its sweet message,
   "First God go and meet in prayer."

Yes, "God First" must be our motto
   If we would succeed each day;
Wish we all our ways to prosper
   Then about them we must pray.

Dear friend, won't you have this motto
   Put up in your room as well?
That to you its own sweet message,
   It may daily, hourly, tell?

Yes, let "God First" be our motto,
   Let it help you to prepare
For life's duties, cares and pleasures,
   By a word with Him in prayer.

I have told you how it helps me,
   It will help you, too, I'm sure;
Fruit through it will be abundant,
   Fruit which ever will endure.   —*A. M. Terry*

PRAYER AT EVENTIDE

For hasty word and secret sin
For needful task undone,
We pray Thy full forgiveness, Lord,
At setting sun.

The day to us has beauty brought,
Thy smile has blessed our way,
Now as the evening hours come
For rest we pray.

Keep us beneath Thy wings tonight
Where peace alone is found,
For in Thy love we rest secure
Thy arms around.

And when tomorrow's duties call,
With joy or sorrow sown,
May we in full surrender seek
Thy will alone.   Amen.

                    —*Bob Jones, Jr.*

My Prayer—God's Answer

I prayed for strength, and then I lost awhile
    All sense of nearness, human and divine;
The love I leaned on failed and pierced my heart,
    The hands I clung to loosed themselves from mine;
But while I swayed, weak, trembling, and alone,
    The everlasting arms upheld my own.

I prayed for light; the sun went down in clouds,
    The moon was darkened by a misty doubt;
The stars of heaven were dimmed by earthly fears,
    And all my little candle flames burned out;
But while I sat in shadow, wrapped in night,
    The face of Christ made all the darkness light.

I prayed for peace, and dreamed of restful ease,
    A slumber drugged from pain, a hushed repose;
Above my head the skies were black with storm,
    And fiercer grew the onslaught of my foes;
But while the battle raged, and wild winds blew,
    I heard His voice and perfect peace I knew.

I thank Thee, Lord, Thou wert too wise to heed
    My feeble prayers, and answer as I sought,
Since these rich gifts Thy bounty has bestowed
    Have brought me more than all I asked or thought;
Giver of good, so answer each request
    With Thine own giving, better than my best.
                —*Annie Johnson Flint*

(Copyright by Evangelical Publishers, Toronto, Canada)

Choose Thou for Me

Thy will, dear Lord, I pray, not mine,
    For I could never choose aright;
My future path I cannot see,
    With this my dim and earthly sight.

Choose Thou for me, O Lord, I ask
    Whatever seemeth good to Thee;
For I would rather rest in faith,
    And, like a child, just trustful be.

I am afraid that I would choose
    The smoothest path and bluest sky;
So I would never, 'midst the storms,
    Hear that sweet whisper, "It is I."

And I would ask, I know right well,
    A life without one single care;
Thus I would lose the soothing balm
    Of coming oft to Thee in prayer.

A life without one cloud to hide
    The brightness of that azure sky;
Without one heart-pang or a grief,
    And ne'er one bitter, helpless cry.

But Thou, O Lord, Thou knowest all,
    Thou knowest what I need the best;
I'll take with joy the pleasant things,
    And Thy sweet will shall choose the rest.
          —*M. E. Rae*

GOD OF THE GALLANT TREES

God of the gallant trees
    Give to us fortitude;
Give as Thou givest to these
    Valorous hardihood.
We are the trees of Thy planting, O God,
    We are the trees of Thy wood.

Now let the life-sap run
    Clean through our every vein;
Perfect that Thou hast begun,
    God of the sun and rain;
Thou who dost measure the weight of the wind
    Fit us for stress and for strain.
          —*Amy Carmichael*

I Thank Thee Now, Dear Lord

I thank Thee now, dear Lord,
That Thou didst plough into my heart
So heavily; Thou sawest the tares
Had such root taken unawares,
The wheat had lost its early start
And sterile grew my stony heart.

I thank Thee now, dear Lord,
For gusty clouds in cheerless sky,
For gentle showers that pattering fell,
For rainbows flashed o'er field and dell;
Thou didst plan for harvest by and by,
The while I thought Thou wert not nigh.

I thank Thee now, dear Lord,
That Thou didst sow the harrowed field
Anew, so seeds of tenderness
Could burst for others in distress,
And my dumb lips become unsealed
To praise Thee for Thy love revealed.

—Grace W. Haight

Prayer

Prayer is the soul's desire to God
    Which must forever be
According to His precious Word—
    Marked with humility.

God's ear is ever open to
    The humble cry and plea;
He takes account of each desire—
    Helps each infirmity.

The heart that's cleansed from sin will feel
    God's gracious Presence near;
Accepted in His Precious Son
    With nothing, then, to fear.

Prayer must be grounded on the Word
    Accompanied with faith
Thus, what's according to His will
    God answers—as He saith.

God never fails to answer prayer
    In fervency implored;
So, let each need presented be
    Before our gracious Lord.

If these conditions be fulfilled
    God's blessing will impart
Fulness of joy, and faith, and love
    To every waiting heart.

                    —*M. E. H.*

LISTENING IN

"God has a wireless to everywhere,
We call it the word of God and prayer;
And everyone may daily win
God's choicest gifts by listening in.

First you must shut out every sound
From the heedless world that throngs around;
'Vanity Fair' makes a deafening din
On purpose to hinder listening in.

The devil will use his utmost power
To keep you from having this quiet hour;
He knows that you can be freed from sin
Always and only by listening in.

But when you carefully read God's word,
The still, small voice is clearly heard;
And wondrous peace and power within
Daily result from listening in.

God longs to give His best to you,
To keep you loyal, strong, and true;
If you haven't begun, today begin
To prove the joy of listening in."

Make Me Strong and True

"God, who touchest earth with beauty,
  Make me lovely, too,
With thy Spirit recreate me;
  Make my heart anew.

Like thy springs and running waters,
  Make me crystal pure;
Like thy rocks of towering grandeur,
  Make me strong and sure.

Like thy dancing waves in sunlight,
  Make me glad and free;
Like the straightness of the pine trees,
  Let me upright be.

Like the arching of the heavens
  Lift my thoughts above;
Turn my dreams to noble action,
  Ministries of love.

God, who touchest earth with beauty,
  Make me lovely, too;
Keep me ever, by thy Spirit,
  Pure, and strong, and true."

A Morning Prayer

I ask thee not to withhold grief
Thou hast in store for me;
I only ask for courage, Lord,
  To bear it patiently.

To always tread the flowery path?
Not this my earnest plea;
I only ask my hand in thine,
  Then I'll wait patiently.

I pray thee not to smooth one wave
From off my troubled sea;
Only give my frail bark strength
　　To sail through patiently.

I ask thee not to always place
Sweet fruit upon life's tree,
But of the bitter fruit—dear Lord,
　　To partake patiently.

Some day the azure sky will break
And Thy dear face I'll see;
I pray that Thou wilt find me, Lord,
　　Waiting patiently.

　　　　　　　　　　　　—*Betty Perpetuo*

A Prayer for Revival

"Lord, send revival,"
　　The prophets of old did pray,
When earth was shrouded in darkness,
　　And they could not find their way.

Lord, send Thy power,
　　Let it descend on us now,
Stir our hearts, we pray Thee,
　　In Thy presence we humbly bow.

Lord, send Thy Spirit
　　To convict us all of sin;
Help us to remove every hindrance,
　　Show us where to begin.

The world is filled with sadness,
　　With sorrow, pain, and woe;
Millions are walking blindly
　　Not knowing whither they go.

Give us a deep-burning passion,
　　Teach us the meaning of "Lost,"
Help us to win the poor sinners,
　　To reach them, whatever the cost.

Send us to city and country,
    To radio, church, and the street;
Help us to give the true Gospel
    That leads to Thy pierced feet.

Help us to tell the old story,
    How the Savior suffered and died,
How the thief who hung there beside Him
    Was saved when for mercy he cried.

Help us to live every moment
    As in the sight of His eye,
That others may follow us upward
    To dwell with our Savior on high.

Lord, send a world-wide revival,
    Whatever the cost may be;
Lord, send a mighty revival,
    And let it begin in me.

—Clifford Lewis

Pray—Give—Go

Three things the Master hath to do
    And we who serve Him here below
And long to see His Kingdom come
    May Pray or Give or Go.

He needs them all—the Open Hand,
    The Willing Feet, the Praying Heart—
To work together, and to weave
    A three-fold cord that shall not part.

Nor shall the giver count his gift
    As greater than the worker's deed,
Nor he in turn his service boast
    Above the prayers that voice the need.

Not all can Go; not all can Give,
    To speed the message on its way,
But young or old, or rich or poor,
    Or strong or weak—we all can Pray:

Pray that the gold-filled hands may Give
  To arm the others for the fray;
That those who hear the call may Go,
  And pray—that other hearts may Pray!
                     —*Annie Johnson Flint*

BECAUSE YOU PRAYED

Because you prayed for me
I found the strength I needed for my task,
The courage I lacked before, the faith to see
Beyond my narrow world; new joy for pain
I found, and zeal
To press on forward strong of heart again—
Because you prayed.

Because you prayed today
I found it was not hard to face the dawn,
Take up again the work I laid away
But yesterday, and shoulder it, and dare
To smile a bit
And find a blessing I'd not dreamed was there—
Because you prayed.

Because you prayed for me
Tonight, I seemed to reach and find your hand
Close by as I had known it would be,
And somehow toil and turmoil needs must cease:—
It was as though
God to our hearts had softly whispered, "Peace"—
Because you prayed.
                     —*Ruth Margaret Gibbs*

LITTLE HATTIE'S CHAIR

The day that little Hattie died
 The house seemed strange and queer;
The furniture looked different,
 And everything was drear;
We children all would huddle close
 Upon the steps and try
To think of Heaven where she was,
 And then we all would cry.

Then Bobbie sneaked off by himself,
 And we hunted everywhere
Till Father found him in the yard
 In little Hattie's chair;
He was hid behind the lilac bush
 Where she would often play,
And his face was streaked with tears
 And he called, "Oh, keep away."

But Father kissed him on the head
 And lifted chair and all
And carried him into the house
 And on up through the hall;
Until he reached the attic door,
 And we kept following, too,
Because we wondered what it was
 That he was going to do.

He got a hammer and a nail
 And drove it 'way up high,
And said, "Now, children, you may kiss
 The little chair good-bye;
But you must never take it down
 And never sit on it"—
And there stood Mother, watching us—
 And we all cried a bit.

One Saturday when Bobbie was
    A-tracking to its lair,
A wild beast of the forest,
    He climbed the attic stair—
Quite softly in his stocking feet
    And peeped in through the door,
And there by little Hattie's chair
    Knelt Mother on the floor.

"Oh Jesus, spare the others—
    And make them pure and good,
Help me to train them carefully
    As a Christian mother should";
Then Bobbie tiptoed down the stairs
    And told us what he'd heard,
And we looked at one another
    But didn't speak a word.

That evening after Father came,
    And we got the song books out,
And took our turn in reading
    A Bible verse about;
He said he'd heard that we had been
    So very good all day,
But no one told him 'twas because
    Bobbie heard Mother pray.

                        —*Grace W. Haight*

Prayer Changes Things

Skies seemed dark to me one morning
And my thoughts were tinged with gloom,
But my eye fell on a motto
That was hanging in the room;
Silvery letters in blue back-ground
Heavenly thought on shining wings,
Brought me hope in one brief message;
It was this: "Prayer changes things!"

Things surround like iron mountains
Things that make a thorny way,
Things that curtain clouds with doubting,
Things that make it hard to pray;
Dreadful things that never happen
Dog our steps, but faith still sings,
In our ears this hopeful message,
"Don't forget: Prayer changes things!"

We have seen some things prayer changes,
Greater things we yet may see,
When the Hebrews came from Egypt
Prayer made pathways through the sea;
In the hot and dusty desert
Moses prayed, and cooling springs
Gushed out from their rocky prisons,
Just because: "Prayer changes things!"

We should be so very careful
Lest some things should change our prayers,
Pleasing things like lotus perfumes
Steal in on us unawares;
Till we loiter in a dreamland,
Slaves but thinking we are kings,
There's a golden key to freedom,
It is this: "Prayer changes things!"

When we think that our surroundings
Keep us from the heavenly way,
Or that wealth or chance will help us
In some distant place or day;
Let's remember 'tis our Savior,
Not environment, that brings
Strength and blessing, peace and pleasure,
Here's the way: "Prayer changes things!"

—*Raymond Browning*

God Answers Prayer

"I know not by what methods rare,
But this I know, God answers prayer;
I know that He has given His word,
Which tells me prayer is always heard,
And will be answered, soon or late;
And so I pray, and calmly wait.

I know not if the blessing sought
Will come in just the way I thought;
But leave my prayers with Him alone,
Whose will is wiser than my own,
Assured that He will grant my quest,
Or send some answer far more blest."

As a Child to Its Father

My grateful thanks, dear Lord, because today
While I within my room prepared to pray,
Before my lips had formed the spoken word
I knew my needs were met and you had heard.

How strange to kneel so lonely, so afraid
And then to rise refreshed and undismayed!
You gave no outward sign that I could see,
And yet I felt your love surrounding me.

And now my wilderness is filled with bread,
And I may walk as one divinely led.

—*Eugenia T. Finn*

SALVATION

The Life That Pays

It pays to be a Christian,
  It pays in every way
To know the blessed Savior
  And trust Him day by day.

The world will always fail you,
  No matter where you go,
Sin always leads to sorrow,
  To sadness and to woe.

Christ died upon the cross
  To save your soul from sin;
Open now the door by faith,
  He'll gladly enter in.

He'll answer all your questions,
  He'll surround you with His care,
He'll solve your every problem,
  Your heavy burdens bear.

He understands completely,
  He listens when we call;
Our everlasting portion,
  Christ lifts us when we fall.

He'll never, never, leave us,
  A blessed fact to know;
So we'll live for Him completely
  As heavenward we go.

—Clifford Lewis

In the Depths of the Sea

"I will cast in the depths of the fathomless sea
All your sins and transgressions whatever they be;
Though they mount up to heaven, though they reach down to hell,
They shall sink into depths, and above them shall dwell
All my waves of forgiveness so mighty and free;
I will cast all your sins in the depths of the sea.

In the deep, silent depths far away from the shore,
Where they never may rise to trouble thee more,
Where no far-reaching tide with its pitiless sweep
May stir the dark waves of forgetfulness deep,
I have buried them there where no mortal can see;
I have cast all your sins in the depths of the sea."

The Touch of the Master's Hand

"'Twas battered and scarred, and the auctioneer
    Thought it scarcely worth his while
To waste much time on the old violin,
    But he held it up with a smile;
'What am I bidden, good folk?' he cried,
    'Who'll start the bidding for me?
A dollar—one dollar—then two, only two—
    Two dollars, and who'll make it three?
Going for three'—but no—
    From the room far back, a grayhaired man
Came forward and picked up the bow;
    Then wiping the dust from the old violin,
And tightening the loosened strings,
    He played a melody pure and sweet
    As a caroling angel sings.

The music ceased and the auctioneer,
    With a voice that was quiet and low,
Said, 'Now what am I bid for the old violin?'
    And he held it up with the bow;
'A thousand dollars—and who'll make it two?
    Two thousand and who'll make it three?
Three thousand once—three thousand twice—
    And going—and gone,' cried he;
The people cheered, but some of them cried,
    'We do not understand;
What changed its worth?' Quick came the reply,
    'The touch of a master's hand.'

And many a man with life out of tune,
  And battered and scarred with sin,
Is auctioned cheap to a thoughtless crowd,
  Much like the old violin,
A mess of pottage—a glass of wine,
  A game—and he travels on;
He's going once—and going twice—
  He's going—and almost gone!
But the Master comes, and the foolish crowd
  Never can quite understand,
The worth of a soul, and the change that's wrought
  BY THE TOUCH OF THE MASTER'S HAND."

IN HIM NO DARKNESS

"Let there be light," God said;
And lo! across the chasm of the deep
  All darkness fled
  Dismayed before the One
Whose radiance outshines a noonday sun;
  And dawn came on,
  And morning out of night,
When God, sweeping across the chaos, said,
  "Let there be light!"

"Let there be light," God said;
And lo! from out my sinful heart
  The darkness fled;
  From bondage I was free.
I only looked in faith to Calvary,
  Saw One and loved Him;
  Thus I gained my sight
When God swept down across my soul, and said,
  "Let there be light!"

                    —*Ruth Margaret Gibbs*

SIN AND ITS CURE

"The worst of all diseases
　　Is light compared with sin;
On every part it seizes,
　　But rages most within.
'Tis palsy, plague, and fever,
　　And madness all combined;
And none but a believer
　　The least relief can find.

From men great skill professing
　　I thought a cure to gain,
But this proved more distressing,
　　And added to my pain.
Some said that nothing ailed me,
　　Some gave me up for lost;
Thus every refuge failed me,
　　And all my hopes were crossed.

At length the Great Physician—
　　How matchless is His grace,
Accepted my petition,
　　And undertook my case.
First gave me sight to view Him—
　　For sin my eyes had sealed,
Then bid me look unto Him;
　　I looked, and I was healed!"

HE SAVES, KEEPS, AND SATISFIES

His Blood Takes My Sin Away

"The blood of Jesus Christ His Son cleanseth us from all sin."
I John 1:7

"All my sins I lay on Jesus!
　　He doth wash me in His blood;
He will keep me pure and holy,
　　He will bring me home to God."

His Word Takes My Doubt Away

"These things have I written unto you that believe on the name of the Son of God; that ye may know that ye have eternal life, and that ye may believe on the name of the Son of God."
I John 5:13

"All my doubts I give to Jesus!
   I've His gracious promise heard;
I shall never be confounded—
   I am trusting in His word."

His Love Takes My Fear Away

"There is no fear in love; but perfect love casteth out fear: because fear hath torment. He that feareth is not made perfect in love." I John 4:18

"All my fears I give to Jesus!
   Rests my weary soul on Him;
Though my way be hid in darkness,
   Never can His light grow dim."

OUR NEED

This land is filled with much sorrow,
   And Christ looking down from above
Must weep when He sees our condition,
   Men spurning His wonderful love.

There are many around who are homeless,
   Nothing with which to buy bread;
We see those whose garments are threadbare,
   How blessed if they could be fed.

Not only their bodies are hungry,
   Their souls are perishing too,
Because some will not trust the dear Savior,
   Who only can give life anew.

Many have great earthly riches,
　　And are striving with all of their might
To add to their worldly possessions,
　　But still they are poor in God's sight.

Let's go out and tell all the sinners
　　How Jesus has died in their stead,
How the grave became our Lord's victim,
　　Because He arose from the dead.

He ascended to be with the Father
　　And is now interceding above;
He is coming to take us to glory,
　　Because we've been saved through His love.

　　　　　　　　　　　　—Clifford Lewis

INVITATION AND RESPONSE

"Come unto Me," the Savior said
　　And I will give thee rest,
Thy heart I'll free from fear and dread
　　And guide thee for the best.

I take Thy rest, O Christ of God
　　Forgiveness from all sin,
For Thou hast shed Thy precious blood
　　Deep peace to give within.

Come, weary, heavy-laden heart
　　Cast all thy care on Me,
Peace from thy soul shall not depart
　　But last eternally.

I cast my every care on Thee
　　In confidence sublime,
Knowing that Thou wilt care for me
　　Through all the years of time.

Nor will *time* end Thy care, Thy love,
　　But fellowship divine
Shall still be ours in Heaven above
　　And all the glory Thine.

　　　　　　　　　　　　—M. E. H.

I Take—He Undertakes

I clasp the hand of Love divine,
I claim the gracious promise mine
And add to His my countersign,
    I take — He undertakes.

Chorus

I take Thee, blessed Lord,
    I give myself to Thee,
And Thou, according to Thy word,
    Dost undertake for me.

I take salvation full and free,
Through Him who gave His life for me,
He undertakes my all to be,
    I take — He undertakes.

I take Him as my holiness,
My spirit's spotless, heavenly dress,
I take the Lord, my righteousness,
    I take — He undertakes.

I take the promised Holy Ghost,
I take the power of Pentecost
To fill me to the uttermost,
    I take — He undertakes.

I take Him for this mortal frame,
I take my healing through His name,
And all His risen life I claim,
    I take — He undertakes.

I simply take Him at His word,
I praise Him that my prayer is heard,
And claim my answer from the Lord,
    I take — He undertakes.

                      —A. B. Simpson

Jesus Paid It All!

"Nothing to pay?—no, not a whit;
Nothing to do? no, not a bit;
All that was needed to do or to pay,
Jesus has done in His own blessed way.

Nothing to do? no, not a stroke!
Gone is the captor, gone is the yoke;
Jesus at Calvary severed the chain,
And none can imprison His freeman again.

Nothing to fear? no, not a jot;
Nothing unclean—no, not a spot;
Christ is my peace, and I've nothing at stake,
Satan can neither harass nor shake.

Nothing to settle?—all has been paid;
Nothing of anger?—peace has been made:
Jesus alone is the sinner's resource,
Peace He has made by the blood of His cross.

What about judgment?—I'm thankful to say,
Jesus has met it and borne it away;
Drank it all up, when He hung on the tree,
Leaving a cup full of blessing for me.

What about terror?—it hasn't a place
In a heart that is filled with a sense of His grace;
My peace is divine and it never can cloy,
And that makes my heart over-bubble with joy.

Nothing of guilt—no, not a stain,
How could the blood let any remain?
My conscience is purged, and my spirit is free—
Precious that blood is to God and to me!

What of the law?—ah, there I rejoice,
Christ answered its claims and silenced its voice;
The law was fulfilled when the work was all done,
And it ne'er can condemn a justified one.

What about death?—it hasn't a sting;
The grave to a Christian no terror can bring,
For death has been conquered, the grave has been spoiled,
And every foeman and enemy foiled.

What about feelings?—ah! trust not to them;
What of my standing—Who shall condemn?
Since God is for me there is nothing so clear,
From Satan and man I have nothing to fear.

What of my body?—ah! that I may bring
To God as a holy, acceptable thing,
For that is the temple where Jesus abides,
The temple where God by His Spirit resides.

Nothing to pay, no, thanks be to God,
The matter is settled, the price was the blood,
The blood of the victim, a ransom divine—
Believe it, poor sinner, and peace shall be thine.

What am I waiting for? Jesus, my Lord,
To take down the tent and roll up the cord—
To be with Himself in the mansion above,
Enjoying forever His infinite love."

SECOND COMING

Thy Kingdom Come

O Christ my Lord and King,
    This is the prayer I bring;
This is the song I sing,
    Thy kingdom come.

Help me to work and pray,
    Help me to live each day,
That all I do may say,
    Thy kingdom come.

Upon my heart's high throne
    Rule Thou, and Thou alone;
Let me be all Thine own;
    Thy kingdom come.

Through all the earth abroad,
    Wherever man has trod,
Send forth Thy word, O God;
    Thy kingdom come.

Soon may our King appear,
    Haste, bright Millennial Year;
We live to bring it near;
    Thy kingdom come.

—A. B. Simpson

The Cross and Crown

With burdened heart and soul our Savior bore
The cruel cross—alone—to Calvary;
Is it too much to bear thy heavy cross,
Until, in glory's crown, He comes for thee?

They pressed the crown of thorns upon His brow;
His precious blood was shed—now thou art free;
Is it too much to wear thy thorny crown,
Until the King of Kings shall come for thee?

Nay, say not they are burdensome to bear!
So very soon thy cross thou wilt lay down;
The morning light now gleams in eastern skies;
Soon thou shalt wear, with Him, the victor's crown.

'Twill be in glory's crown, not with a cross,
Our Victor will return, His battle won;
'Tis just a little while, oh waiting soul,
Until thine eyes behold God's only Son.

—Betty Perpetuo

JERUSALEM

Jerusalem! Jerusalem!
    To me forever dear!
My very heart doth melt with love
    When thy sweet name I hear.
I love thy very walls and towers,
    That many a tale could tell;
I love thy valleys and thy hills;
    I love, I love thee well.

But most of all, I love thee well
    Because the Son of God
So oft o'er all these sacred scenes
    With holy footsteps trod.
The halo of His presence still
    Seems lingering all around,
And every spot my footsteps tread,
    Is sacred, hallowed ground.

But one sweet spot is dearer far
    Than all the rest to me;
A low green hill hard by thy walls,
    The place called Calvary.
Nay, there's another spot I hold
    With love that's fonder yet,
Where last His blessed footsteps trod,—
    The Mount of Olivet.

Methinks the very smile of heaven
    Is ever lingering here;
Methinks the very angel hosts
    Are ever hovering near.
I sat upon that mountain side
    O'erlooking Bethany,
And never shall my heart forget
    What Jesus said to me.

It was not words, it was not thoughts,
    'Twas just a breath of love;
But something to my heart it meant,
    All thoughts and words above.
Yet this I know that message meant—
    That soon He'll come again—
Oh, blessed hope! Our glorious King
    Will soon begin His reign!

Jerusalem! Jerusalem!
    Forever dear to me!
While life and love and God shall live,
    I will remember thee!   —*A. B. Simpson*

STIR ME

Stir me, O stir me, Lord, till all my heart
Is filled with strong compassion for these souls,
Till Thy compelling "Must" drives me to pray,
Till Thy constraining Love reach to the poles,
Far North and South, in burning deep desire,
Till East and West are caught in Love's great fire.

Stir me, O stir me, Lord, Thy heart was stirred
By Love's intensest fire, till Thou didst give
Thine Only Son, Thy best beloved One,
Even to the dreadful Cross, that I might live;
Stir me to give myself so back to Thee,
That Thou canst give Thyself again through me.

Stir me, O stir me, Lord, for I can see
Thy glorious triumph day begin to break!
The dawn already gilds the eastern sky;
Oh, Church of Christ, arise! awake! awake!
Oh, stir us, Lord, as heralds of that day,
For night is past—our King is on His way!
                    —*Bessie Porter Head*

TEMPERANCE

DON'T DRINK!

Little drops of alcohol
    Make a man a fool,
Make him miss the bridges—
    Drive into the pool!

Little drops of beer and
    Wine in daddy's head,
Coaxed off the money
    For shoes and clothes and bread!

Little drops of liquor
    Swallowed, through the years,
Make a mother sadder,
    Fill her eyes with tears!

So we'll never drink it,
    The horrid, nasty scum,
Nor tote a whisky-bottle
    That makes a man a bum!

—*Mrs. Thos. Stetten*

BOOZERS AND PIGS

"One evening in October,
    When I was far from sober
And dragging home a load with manly pride,
    My poor feet began to stutter,
So I laid down in the gutter
    And a pig came up and parked right by my side.

Then I warbled, 'It's fair weather
    When good fellows get together,'
Till a lady passing by was heard to say,
    'You can tell a man who boozes
By the playmates that he chooses,'
    Then the pig got up and quickly ran away."

ISN'T IT STRANGE!

"I have walked in summer meadows
    Where the sunbeams flashed and broke,
But I never saw the cattle
    Or any of the horses smoke.

I have watched the birds with wonder
    When the world with dew is wet,
But I never saw a robin
    Puffing at a cigarette.

I have fished in many a river
    Where the sucker crop is ripe,
But I never saw a catfish
    Puffing at a briar pipe.

Man's the only living creature
    That blows where'r he goes,
Like a booming tractor engine,
    Smoke from mouth and nose.

If God had intended he would smoke
    When He first invented man,
He would have built him on
    A widely different plan.

He'd have fixed him with a stovepipe,
    A damper and a grate,
And he'd had a smoke consumer
    That was strictly up-to-date."

A FILTHY WEED

"Tobacco is a filthy weed,
It was the devil who sowed the seed;
It picks your pockets, spoils your clothes,
And makes a chimney out of your nose.

It costs to use this filthy weed,
This good advice I hope you'll heed;
Don't touch again the poison stuff,
Because, you know, you've had enough.

If you've never used this filthy weed,
Don't start it now, there is no need;
Keep body clean, your mind keep bright,
And you'll be glad you decided right."

VICTORY!

You cannot do the thing that's right
    Without the Christ within;
He'll turn your darkness into light,
    He, only, saves from sin.

You can have His strength from day to day,
    Say "No" to bad habits and sin;
When Satan tries to lead you astray,
    Pray hard and the victory win.

You can have each moment His mighty power,
    Look full in His wonderful face;
He'll deliver you this very hour,
    Trust Him and His matchless grace.
                              —*Clifford Lewis*

THANKSGIVING

I Give Thee Humble Thanks

For all the gifts that Thou dost send,
For every kind and loyal friend,
For prompt supply of all my need,
For all that's good in word or deed,
For gift of health along life's way,
For strength to work from day to day,
    I give Thee humble thanks.

For ready hands to help and cheer,
For list'ning ears Thy voice to hear,
For yielded tongue Thy love to talk,
For willing feet Thy paths to walk,
For open eyes Thy word to read,
For loving heart thy will to heed,
    I give Thee humble thanks.

For Christ who came from heaven above,
For the cross and His redeeming love,
For His mighty power to seek and save,
For His glorious triumph o'er the grave,
For the lovely mansions in the sky,
For His blessed coming bye and bye,
    I give Thee humble thanks.

—Clifford Lewis

The Blessings that Remain

There are loved ones who are missing
    From the fireside and the feast;
There are faces that have vanished,
    There are voices that have ceased;
But we know they passed forever
    From our mortal grief and pain,
And we thank Thee, O our Father,
    For the blessings that remain.

Thanksgiving, oh, thanksgiving,
   That their love once blessed us here,
That so long they walked beside us,
   Sharing every smile and tear;
For the joy the past has brought us,
   But can never take away,
For the sweet and gracious memories
   Growing dearer every day.

For the faith that keeps us patient
   Looking at the things unseen,
Knowing Spring shall follow Winter
   And the earth again be green,
For the hope of that glad meeting
   Far from mortal grief and pain—
We thank Thee, O our Father,
   For the blessings that remain.

—Annie Johnson Flint

(Copyright by Evangelical Publishers, Toronto, Canada.)

I Give My Thanks to Thee

For every blessing Thou art giving,
For power to hear and talk and see,
For strength to make an honest living,
Lord, I give my thanks to Thee.

For Thy overcoming power,
For Thy blood that ransomed me,
For Thy peace this very hour,
Lord, I give my thanks to Thee.

For Thy mercy everlasting,
For Thy love so full and free,
For Thy grace that's all-sufficient,
Lord, I give my thanks to Thee.

For the hope that Thou hast given,
Thou art coming soon for me,
Take me to my home in heaven,
Lord, I give my thanks to Thee.

—Clifford Lewis

THE TONGUE

Don't Worry About Gossip

We may get through this world, but 'twill be very slow,
If we listen to all that is said as we go,
We'll be worried and fretted and kept in a stew,
For meddlesome tongues must have something to do—
   For people will talk, you know.

If quiet and modest, you'll have it presumed
That your humble position is only assumed;
You're a wolf in sheep's clothing, or else you're a fool,
But don't get excited, keep perfectly cool—
   For people will talk, you know.

If generous and noble, they'll vent out their spleen,
You'll hear some loud hints that you're selfish and mean;
If upright and honest and fair as the day,
They'll call you a rogue in a sly, sneaking way—
   For people will talk, you know.

And then if you show the least boldness of heart,
Or a slight inclination to take your own part,
They will call you an upstart, conceited, and vain,
But keep straight ahead, don't stop to explain—
   For people will talk, you know.

If threadbare your coat, or old-fashioned your hat,
Someone, of course, will take notice of that,
And hint very strong that you can't pay your way,
But don't get excited, whatever they say—
   For people will talk, you know.

If you dress in fashion, don't think to escape,
For they'll criticize then, in a different shape,
You're ahead of your means, or your tailor's unpaid,
But mind your own business, there's naught to be said—
   For people will talk, you know.

If a fellow but chance to converse with a girl,
How gossips will talk, and their scandal unfurl,
They'll canvass your wants, or talk of your means,
And declare you're engaged to a chit in her teens—
    For people will talk, you know.

They'll talk fine before you, but then at your back,
Of venom and slander there's never a lack,
How kind and polite in all that they say,
But bitter as gall when you're out of the way—
    For people will talk, you know.

The best way to do is to always do right,
And at last you will always win out in the fight,
Of course, you will meet with all sorts of abuse,
But don't think to stop them, it is not any use—
    For people will talk, you know.
               —*Samuel Dodge*

TALK ABOUT YOUR NEIGHBOR

"Let us talk about our neighbors;
    Talk of them where'er we go;
Talk about our friend and brother,
    And of everyone we know.
Let us talk about our kindred,
    Spread the news both near and far,
Till the whole town hears the story
    Of what splendid folks they are.

Let us talk about our neighbors;
    Of the kindly deeds they do;
Of the little acts of kindness
    Which they do for me—for you.
Tell about the hours of watching
    Through the night with you in pain;
Of the words of cheer and courage
    When your struggles all seem vain.

Let us talk about our neighbors,
  In the home or at our work,
Where the conversation's cheerful
  Or where germs of envy lurk.
Let us talk about our neighbors,
  But let's be as neighbors should—
Let's not talk about their failures—
  Let us tell of something good."

BE CAREFUL WHAT YOU SAY

In speaking of a person's faults,
  Pray don't forget your own;
Remember those with homes of glass
  Should seldom throw a stone;
If we have nothing else to do,
  But talk of those who sin,
'Tis better we commence at home,
  And from that point begin.

We have no right to judge a man
  Until he's fairly tried;
Should we not like his company,
  We know the world is wide;
Some may have faults—and who has not?
  The old as well as young—
Perhaps we may, for aught we know,
  Have fifty to their one.

I'll tell you of a better plan,
  You'll find it works full well;
To try my own defects to cure
  Before of others' tell;
And though sometimes I hope to be
  No worse than some I know,
My own shortcomings bid me let
  The faults of others go.

Then let us all, when we commence
    To surrender friend or foe,
Think of the harm one word would do
    To those we little know;
Remember, curses, sometimes, like
    Our chickens, "roost at home,"
Don't speak of others' faults until
    We have none of our own.

—*James J. Boucher*

THE TONGUE

" 'The boneless tongue, so small and weak
Can crush and kill,' " declared the Greek;
'The tongue destroys a greater horde,'
The Turk asserts, 'than does the sword.'

The Persian proverb wisely saith;
'A lengthy tongue—an early death';
Or sometimes takes this form instead,
'Don't let your tongue cut off your head.'

'The tongue can speak a word, whose speed'
Says the Chinese, 'outstrips the steed';
While Arab sages this impart:
'The tongue's great storehouse is the heart.'

From Hebrew wit the maxim sprung:
'Though feet may slip, ne'er let the tongue';
The sacred writer crowns the whole:
'Who keeps his tongue, doth keep his soul.' "

UNSELFISHNESS

Others

"Lord, help me live from day to day
   In such a self-forgetful way,
That even when I kneel to pray
   My prayers will be for OTHERS.

"Help me in all the work I do
   To ever be sincere and true,
And know that all I do for YOU
   Must needs be done for OTHERS.

"Let SELF be crucified and slain
   And buried deep, and all in vain
May efforts be to rise again,
   Unless to live for OTHERS.

"And when my work on earth is done
   And my new work in heaven begun,
May I forget the crown I've won
   While thinking still of OTHERS.

"Others, Lord, yes, others—
   Let this my motto be;
Help me to live for OTHERS
   That I may live like Thee."

—*C. D. Meigs*

The Two Temples

"A builder builded a temple,
   He wrought it with grace and skill;
Pillars and groins and arches—
   All fashioned to work his will.

And men said they saw its beauty,
   'It shall never know decay;
Great is thy skill, O builder!
   Thy fame shall endure for aye.'

A teacher builded the temple
  With loving and infinite care;
Planning each arch with patience,
  Laying each stone with prayer.

None praised unceasing efforts,
  None knew of the wondrous plan;
But the temple the teacher builded
  Was unseen by the eye of man.

Gone is the builder's temple,
  Crumbled into dust;
Low lies each stately pillar,
  Food for the consuming rust.

But the temple the teacher builded
  Will last while the ages roll;
For the beautiful unseen temple
  Was a child's immortal soul."

IF I WOULD BE MY BEST

I cannot be, by half, the man I should
  If jealousy finds favor at my door,
For jealousy but mocks another's good
  And sets my heart on what I should ignore.
If I would be each day and hour my best
This canker must not lodge within my breast.

I cannot do, by half, the things I should
  If envy twines its roots about my soul;
For envy seeks but death to brotherhood
  And sets my eyes on some ignoble goal.
If I would do each day and hour my best
This foe to good must leave at my request.

But I can be and do whate'er I should
  If love for others overflows my heart;
For love will act just as the Master would,
  Bid carnal thoughts forever to depart.
Since I would be and do each day my best
The Christ of love shall ever be my guest.
                              —*O. A. Newlin*

Tell Him Now

If with pleasure you are viewing
Any work a man is doing,
If you like him or you love him, tell him now;
Don't withhold your approbation
Till the parson makes oration,
    And he lies with snowy lilies o'er his brow.

For, no matter how you shout it,
He won't really care about it,
He won't know how many teardrops you have shed;
If you think some praise is due him,
Now's the time to slip it to him,
    For he cannot read the tombstone when he's dead.

More than fame and more than money
Is the comment kind and sunny,
And the hearty, warm approval of a friend;
For it gives in life a savor,
It makes you stronger, braver,
    And it gives you heart and courage to the end.

If he earns your praise, bestow it,
If you like him, let him know it,
Let the words of true encouragement be said;
Do not wait till life is over,
And he's underneath the clover,
    For he cannot read the tombstone when he's dead.
                     —*F. W. Brazier*

Write Them a Letter Tonight

"Don't be selfish in things you do,
    But stay in your room tonight;
Deny yourself to the friends that call,
    And a good long letter write.
Write to the dear old folks at home,
    Who sit when the day is done,
With folded hands and downcast eyes,
    And think of the absent one.

Don't selfishly scribble, 'Excuse my haste,
    I've scarcely the time to write,'
Lest their drooping thoughts go wandering back
    To many a bygone night,
When they lost their needed sleep and rest,
    And every breath was a prayer
That God would leave their delicate babe
    To their tender love and care.

Don't let them feel that you've no need
    For their love and counsel wise,
For the heart grows strongly sensitive
    When age has dimmed the eyes;
It might be well to let them believe
    You never forget them quite,
That you deem it a pleasure, when far away,
    Long letters home to write.

Don't think that the young and giddy friends,
    That make your pastime gay,
Have half the anxious thought for you
    That the old folks have today.
The duty of writing, do not put off,
    Let sleep or pleasure wait,
Lest the letter for which they looked and longed
    Be a day or an hour too late;

For the dear old folks at home,
    With locks fast turning white,
Are longing to hear from the absent one;
    Write them a letter tonight!"

THE BRIDGE BUILDER

"An old man, going a lone highway,
Came in the evening, cold and gray,
To a chasm, vast and deep and wide.
The old man crossed in the twilight dim:
The sullen stream had no fears for him;
But he turned when safe on the other side
And built a bridge to span the tide.

'Old man,' said a fellow-pilgrim near,
'You are wasting your strength with building here;
Your journey will end with the ending day,
You never again will pass this way,
You've crossed the chasm, deep and wide;
Why build you this bridge at eventide?'

The builder lifted his old gray head,
'Good friend, in the path I've come,' he said,
'There followeth after me to-day
A youth whose feet must pass this way;
This chasm that has been naught to me,
To that fair-haired youth may a pitfall be;
He, too, must cross in the twilight dim—
Good friend, I am building this bridge for him!' "

APPEAL!

In these last days—when sorrows reign—
    And Israel is oppressed,
May all true Christians still maintain
    God's place of peace and rest.

In Christ alone, such rest is found
    For Gentile, and for Jew,
Daily this proclamation sound
    God's Holy Word is true.

Then hear His voice, true Christian friend,
    And for Jerusalem pray,
God's blessing will your life attend
    And prosper all your way.

Peace then shall be within thy walls,
    Prosperity abound;
"Oh, love the Jew," our Saviour calls,
    With love that is profound.

The "Inasmuch" of Christ abides
    For all who would do well
In ministry—'mid rising tides—
    To His loved Is-ra-el.

—*M. E. H.*

BE PREPARED

The world is in need of you, young folks,
    If your heart is unselfish and true,
If you'll take the Savior to be your guide,
    And trust Him in all that you do;
If you know the Christ who sets men free,
    And with fervor His plans will pursue,
There's a place to be filled in His vineyard today;
    The world is in need of you!

There are all around us leaders galore;
    So many want profit and fame;
There are only a few, compared to the need,
    Who give their best for the name
Of Jesus—Redeemer and Friend,—
    The only hope of Gentile and Jew;
Come, give your service and love to the end,
    The world is in need of you!

Then awake, young folks from your stupor of doubt,
    Trust Jesus your faith to renew;
Don't follow the crowd, but let us resolve
    By His power we'll always be true;
Go, carry His message to those who are lost,
    That's something all Christians should do;
Give Him your best, forgetting the cost,
    The world is in need of you!

—Clifford Lewis

WARNING

Every Christian knows that there is a personal devil. The devil is mighty but God is Almighty. We read in James 4:7 "Submit yourselves therefore to God. Resist the devil, and he will flee from you." Yielded Christians have constant victory over the devil.

The following poem will give the modernists and other unbelievers something to think about:

FAIR QUESTIONS

Men don't believe in a devil now,
As their fathers used to do;
They forced the door of the broadcast creed,
To let his majesty through.
There isn't a print of his cloven foot,
Or a fiery dart from his bow,
To be found in the earth or air today,
For the world has voted it so.

But who is mixing the fatal draught,
That palsies heart and brain,
And loads the bier of passing year
With ten hundred thousand slain;
Who spoils the peace of the world today
With the fiery breath of hell?
If the devil isn't, and never was,
Won't somebody rise and tell:

Who dogs the steps of the toiling saint
And digs the pit for his feet?
Who sows the tares in the field of time
Wherever God sows His wheat?
The devil is voted not to be,
And of course the thing is true,
But who is doing the kind of work,
The devil alone can do?

We are told he does not go around,
Like a roaring lion now,
But whom shall we hold responsible for
The everlasting row
To be heard in home, in church, in state
To the earth's remotest bound,
If the devil, by unanimous vote,
Is nowhere to be found?

164

Won't somebody step to the front,
And make their bow, and show
How the frauds and the crimes of a single day
Spring up; we want to know;
The devil was fairly voted out,
And of course the devil is gone,
But simple people would like to know:
Who carries his business on?

—*Victoria Selin*

A Voice

"Tomorrow, he faithfully promised
Tomorrow for revival I'll pray,
Tomorrow I'll plead as I ought to,
I'm too busy today.

Tomorrow I'll spend in my closet,
Tomorrow I'll humbly bow,
Yet ever a voice was whispering,
'But the church is languishing now.'

Tomorrow, Tomorrow, Tomorrow,
The delay e'er repeated went on,
Tomorrow, Tomorrow, Tomorrow,
Till the years and the Voice were gone.

Till the church its God had forgotten,
Till the land was covered with sin,
Till millions had hopelessly perished,
And eternity was ushered in.

Oh members of the body of Christ,
Oh ye church of the living God,
Oh editors, and leaders and pastors,
Oh saints, where our fathers trod:

The Voice still insistently whispers
Answer not, 'tomorrow I'll pray,'
The voice is one of authority,
The Church needs reviving today."

Darwin's "Origin of Species" is filled with speculations, such as, "We may suppose," and "It may be possible." It is a dangerous thing to believe in evolution. Don't ever let anyone put a doubt into your mind about the Bible. The following poem shows how foolish evolution really is:

EVOLUTION SAYS—

"Once I was a tadpole grubbing in the mire,
Till I became ambitious and started to aspire,
I rubbed my tail so hard against a sunken log,
It disappeared completely and I found myself a frog.

I struggled from my puddle and jumped upon dry land,
And the feeling that was in me, was glorious and grand;
It made me kind o' frisky, so I hopped around a tree
Till I landed in the branches as happy as could be.

And there I spent some aeons, evoluting without fail,
Till I became a monkey and grew another tail;
But still I had ambitions, as the aeons quickly sped,
I climbed down from the tree and walked the earth instead.

My tail got tired with trailing on the hard earth every day,
And twice within my "process" that apendage passed away;
Once again I evoluted, and believe it, if you can,
I awoke one summer morning and found myself—a man!

Now, you tadpoles, in the mire just think what you may be,
If you'll only in your puddles start to climb the family tree;
I'm the genus homo, "finished" for all the world to see,
For when I told my story I was given a D. D."

JONAH AND THE WHALE

"Now listen, my children, I'll tell you a tale,
How old Jonah, the Prophet, got caught by the Whale,
The Whale caught poor Jonah and, bless your dear soul,
He not only caught him but swallowed him whole.

A part of this story is awfully sad,
It is how a big city went to the bad;
When the Lord saw those people with such wicked ways,
He said, "I can't stand them more'n forty more days.

He spoke to old Jonah and said, 'Go and cry
To those hard-hearted people and tell them that I
Give them forty days more to get humbled down,
And if they don't do it, 'I'll tear up their town.'

Jonah heard the Lord speaking and he said, 'No,
That's against my religion and I won't go;
Those Nineveh people ain't nothing to me,
And I am against foreign missions you see.'

He went down to Joppa and there, in great haste,
He boarded a ship for a different place;
The Lord looked down on that ship and said He,
'Old Jonah is fixing to run off from me.'

He set the winds blowing with squeakes and with squeals
And the sea got rowdy and kicked up its heels;
Old Jonah confessed it was all for his sin;
The crew threw him out and the Whale took him in.

The Whale said, 'Old fellow, don't you forget,
I am sent here to take you in out of the wet,
You will get punished aright for your sin,'
So he opened his mouth, and poor Jonah went in.

On beds of green seaweed that fish tried to rest;
He said, 'I will sleep while my food I digest,'
But he got mighty restless and sorely afraid
And he rumbled inside as the old Prophet prayed.

The third day that fish rose up from his bed
With his stomach tore up and a pain in his head;
He said, 'I must get to the air mighty quick,
For this filthy backslider is making me sick.'

He winked his big eyes and wiggled his tail
And pulled for the shore to deliver his male;
He stopped near the shore and looked all around,
And vomited old Jonah right up on the ground.

Old Jonah thanked God for His mercy and grace,
And, turning around to the Whale made a face,
He said, 'After three days I guess you have found
A good man, old fellow, is hard to keep down.'

He stretched himself out with a yawn and a sigh
And sat down in the sun for his clothing to dry;
He thought how much better his preaching would be,
Since from Whale Seminary he had a degree.

When he had rested and dried in the sun,
He started for Nineveh 'most on the run;
He thanked his dear Father in heaven above
For His tender mercy and wonderful love.

And though he was nearly three days late
He preached from the time he entered the gate,
Till the whole population repented and prayed
And the great hand of justice and vengeance was stayed.

Children, when you disobey, remember this tale,
When you run from God's call, look out for the Whale;
There are animals to catch you on sea or on land
And children are swallowed much easier than man."

A Preacher on the Fence

"From out the millions of the earth
    God often calls a man
To preach His Word, and for the truth
    To take a loyal stand.
'Tis sad to see him shun the cross,
    Nor stand in its defense
Between the fields of right and wrong—
    A preacher on the fence.

Before him are the souls of men,
    Destined for heaven or hell;
An open Bible in his hand,
    And yet he dare not tell
Them all the truth as written there;
    He fears the consequence—
The shame of heaven, the joy of hell—
    A preacher on the fence.

Most surely God has called that man
    To battle for the right,
'Tis his to ferret out the wrong
    And turn on us the light.
He standeth not for right nor wrong,
    He feareth an offense,
Great God, deliver us from him—
    That preacher on the fence.

If he should stand up for the wrong,
    The right he'd not befriend;
If he should boldly stand for right,
    The wrong he would offend.
His mouth is closed, he dare not speak
    For freedom or against.
The most disgusting thing on earth—
    A preacher on the fence.

His better judgment, common sense,
    They pull him to the right;
Behold him grip that topmost rail,
    And hold with all his might;
His love of praise, it holds him fast,
    Keeps him from going hence,
Poor man! how fearful will be his plight
    A preacher on the fence."

The Better Way

"It is better to lose with a conscience clean
    Than to win with a trick unfair;
It is better to fail and to know you've been
    Whatever the price was, square,
Than to claim the joy of a far-off goal
    And the cheers of the passerby,
And to know down deep in your inmost soul
    A cheat you must live and die.

Who wins by tricks may take the prize,
    And at first he may think it sweet,
But many a day in the future lies
    When he'll wish he had met defeat;
For the man who lost shall be glad at heart
    And walk with his head up high,
While his conqueror knows he must play the part
    Of a cheat and a living lie.

The prize seems fair when the fight is on,
    But since it is not truly won,
You will hate the thing when the crowds are gone,
    For it stands for a false deed done;
And it's better you never should reach your goal
    Than ever success to buy,
At the price of knowing deep down in your soul
    That your glory is all a lie."

BLESSED IS THE MAN!

As a tree beside the waters with its roots imbedded deep,
    Is the one whom God calls "blessed" in His Word;
But the ones He calls "ungodly" will forever wail and weep,
    Like chaff they shall be scattered, shaken, stirred.

As a leaf that cannot wither are the righteous in His sight,
    Eternally they never will grow old;
But no sinners are permitted to stand upright in the light
    Of His glory that the righteous will enfold.

As a man who always prospers is the way the righteous go,
    The riches of His grace accepting free;
But the way of the ungodly is a way of sin and woe,
    And will perish throughout all eternity.

—*H. H. Savage*

"THOU ART WITH ME"

I sit by the death-bed of a loved one,
    One whom I've loved so long,
My heart is filled with sadness,
    And it seems that I've lost my song.

I have stood in the sick-rooms of many,
    And watched them struggle for breath;
I have heard the gasp in their voices
    As they entered the chamber of death.

I have been in death-cells in prisons,
    Where soon the men had to die;
I have seen them, young, old and hardened,
    With the very death stare in the eye.

I have seen them die in sweet peace
    With a face so serene it did shine;
With some, it seemed they were hearing
    The Master's dear voice, "Come and dine."

With others, I fear as I say it,
    It is sad although it is true,
They seem to be entering darkness,
    With no hope for that home in the blue.

Without Jesus it's dark in the valley,
    He's the Light that shines from above,
He guides us safely while living,
    Points at last to that sweet home of love.

Friend, won't you trust this dear Savior,
    Who came down from His home in the sky
To redeem you and take you to Heaven,
    That place where you'll never more die?

If you'll trust Him, you'll never regret it,
    You'll be happy, content, and secure,
You'll have something that's worth more than money,
    Your peace will forever endure.

—Clifford Lewis

No Time for Jesus

'Mid all the world's mad rush for pleasure,
   Struggle for fame or gold,
Do you not hear the Savior calling?
   Do you His face behold?
Do you not love and serve Him?
   "Too busy!" now, you say;
How could you hope for pardon,
   If Jesus had no time to pray?

Yours is the earth, the sky, the springtime,
   Sunshine and silver rain;
Yours is the whole of God's creation,
   Mountain and growing grain.
Have you no time for Jesus?
   All things to you He gave;
What of your soul's salvation
   If Jesus had no time to save?

For you He lived and loved and suffered,
   Died on the cross of shame;
For you He rose, and waits in glory;
   Can you reject His name?
No time to worship Jesus?
   Centuries rushing by;
What of your life eternal,
   If Jesus had no time to die?

Ringing o'er Galilean waters,
   Pleading from Calv'ry's Hill
Where once the voice of Jesus sounded;
   Oh! hear its echoes still.
"Come unto Me," He's calling
   Down through the ages dim;
For you He waits forever,
   Have you, then, no time for Him?

—Hazel F. Stevens

BEHOLD, I STAND . . . AND KNOCK

—Rev. 3:20

I saw Him come to you last night, dear friend,
When all was silent and your heart was sore;
His face was tender as I saw Him bend
Above the latch key at the outer door.

He gently smiled and paused expectantly
To listen for some welcoming sound within,
Awaiting but your voice to bid Him be
Your guest—Oh! tell me! Did you let Him in?

He was so weary, and His dear hands bore
Traces of nailprints where the spikes were driven—
But yet He carried in those hands rich store
Of living bread for hungry hearts, forgiven,

And water that would bid the thirsty taste
And thirst no more; oh friend, how could your heart,
Knowing of nothing but the desert waste
Refuse, and let this waiting One depart?

I saw Him come as He has come before
To you, and lest He turn to go, I cried:
"Stay, Master! Let me force that stubborn door
That you may dine with this, my friend, inside!"

He did not answer, but I heard Him sigh,
His eyes, compassionate and deep, which said,
"No, child, each chooses for himself, if I
May be his guest, and break with him My bread."
—Ruth Margaret Gibbs

THE FOUR CALLS

"The Spirit came in *childhood*,
    And pleaded, 'Let me in.'
But Oh! the door was bolted,
    By thoughtlessness and sin;
'I am too young,' the child replied,
    'I will not yield today,
There's time enough tomorrow';
    The Spirit went away.

Again He came and pleaded,
    In *youth's* bright happy hour,
He came, but heard no answer,
    For lured by Satan's power,
The youth lay dreaming then,
    And saying, 'Not today,
Nor till I've tried earth's pleasures';
    The Spirit went away.

Again He called in mercy,
    In *manhood's* vigorous prime,
But still he found no welcome,
    The merchant had no time;
No time for true repentance,
    No time to think or pray,
And so, repulsed and saddened,
    The Spirit went away.

Once more He called and waited,
    The man was *old* and ill,
He scarcely heard the whisper,
    His heart was cold and still;
'Go leave me, when I need thee,
    I'll call for thee,' he cried;
Then sinking on his pillow,
    Without a hope, he died."

The March of Time

Time marches on, its hurrying feet
Are sounding down life's busy street;
We listen to their measured beat,
      Time marches on!

Time marches on, its clarion call
Is heard in hut and palace-hall;
Though kingdoms rise and kingdoms fall,
      Time marches on!

Time marches on, nor can it stay
To wipe the orphan's tears away;
Nor grief of anguished hearts allay,
      Time marches on!

Time marches on, its steady flight
Is heralding approaching night;
And though its locks with age are white,
      Time marches on!

Time marches on—'twill end some day,
When heaven and earth shall pass away;
And then forever and for aye—
      ETERNITY!

ETERNITY! and time no more
Shall march along earth's storm-swept shore;
Its toll of years forever o'er—
      ETERNITY.

ETERNITY! where wilt thou spend
That dateless age that has no end?
O haste and make thy choice, my friend,
      Time marches on!

—*M. E. Rae*

THE GAME THAT YOU CAN'T BEAT

There is one game that you can't beat,
    It is the game of sin;
Many have tried it, but they have failed
    Before they had time to begin.

'Tis very foolish to try and act wise
    And trample the law of God;
Sin will ruin, disgrace, and will kill you,
    It will put you under the sod.

Many folks learn when it's too late,
    That better it would have been
To have lived a manly and Christian life,
    Than to have lived their lives in sin.

The transgressor's way is always hard,
    Are words that have ever been true;
Men heard them of old but heeded them not,
    And now they come to us anew.

You cannot beat the game of sin,
    No matter how hard you try;
Nations can't do it, neither can men,
    They're disgraced, they perish and die.

Rome with her splendor, Greece with her pride,
    Babylon, Sodom, and Gomorrah,
Athens with culture, all forgot God,
    And their fall made a picture of horror.

Learning is good, and wealth is not bad,
    Power is desired, we know,
But we must not forget, although it is sad,
    We always reap what we sow.

Sow to the flesh, of the flesh we shall reap
    A harvest of utter damnation,
Ruin to body and ruin to mind,
    And the soul soon comes to starvation.

Life is a very short span at the most,
    So while time so swiftly is flying,
Let us resolve to sow good seed,
    Then we'll have no fear when dying.

We know that the wages of sin is death,
    And that life is a brittle cord,
But the gift of God is Eternal Life
    Through Jesus Christ our Lord.

—Clifford Lewis

A CRY FROM HEATHENDOM

Why didn't you tell us sooner?
    The words came sad and low,
O ye who knew the gospel truths,
    Why didn't you let us know?
The Savior died for those in sin,
    He died to save from woe;
But we never heard the story,
    Why didn't you let us know?

You have had the gospel message,
    You have known a Savior's love,
Your dear ones passed from Christian homes,
    To the blessed land above.
Why did you let our fathers die,
    And into the silence go?
With no thought of Christ to comfort,
    Why didn't you let us know?

We appeal to you, O Christians,
    In lands beyond the sea!
Why didn't you tell us sooner,
    Christ died to set men free?
Nineteen hundred years have passed
    Since disciples were told to go
To the uttermost parts of the earth and teach,
    Why didn't you let us know?

You say you are Christ's disciples—
　　That you try His work to do,
And yet His very last command
　　Is disobeyed by you.
'Tis indeed a wonderful story!
　　He loved the whole world so,
That He came and died to save us,
　　But you didn't let us know!

O souls, redeemed by Jesus,
　　Think what your Lord hath done,
He came to earth and suffered,
　　And died for man undone.
He expected you to tell it,
　　As on your way you go,
But you kept the message from us!
　　Why didn't you let us know?

Hear this pathetic cry of ours,
　　O dwellers in Christian lands!
For heathendom stands before you,
　　With pleading outstretched hands,
You may not be able to come yourself,
　　But some in your stead can go,
Will you not send us teachers?
　　Will you not let us know?"

FIRST THINGS FIRST

No time, no time for study
　　To meditate and pray—
And yet much time for *"doing"*
　　In a fleshly, worldly way.

No time for things Eternal
　　But much for things of earth,
The things important set aside
　　For things of little worth.

Some things, 'tis true, are needful
　　But first things must come first;
And what displaces God's own Word
　　Of God it shall be cursed.

—*M. E. H.*

OUT OF TOUCH

Only a smile, yes, only a smile,
That a woman o'erburdened with grief
Expected from you; 'twould have given relief
For her heart ached sore the while;
But weary and cheerless she went away,
Because, as it happened, that very day
You were "out of touch" with your Lord.

Only a word, yes, only a word,
That the Spirit's small voice whispered, "Speak";
But the worker passed onward, unblessed and weak,
Whom you were meant to have stirred
To courage, devotion and love anew,
Because, when the message came to you,
You were "out of touch" with your Lord.

Only a note, yes, only a note,
For a friend in a distant land;
The Spirit said, "Write," but then you had planned
Some different work, and you thought
It mattered little, you did not know
'Twould have saved a soul from sin and woe;
You were "out of touch" with your Lord.

Only a song, yes, only a song,
That the Spirit said, "Sing to-night—
Thy voice is thy Master's by purchased right";
But you thought, " 'Mid this motley throng
I care not to sing of the City of Gold,"
And the heart that your words might have reached grew cold;
You were "out of touch" with your Lord.

Only a day, yes, only a day!
But, oh can you guess, my friend,
Where the influence reaches, and where it will end
Of the hours that you frittered away?
The Master's command is, "Abide in Me,"
And fruitless and vain will your service be,
If "out of touch" with your Lord.

—Jean H. Watson

Unfit for Service

"One night, 'twas a Saturday evening,
I sat alone in my room,
Watching the fading daylight,
And the steadily gathering gloom,
And I longed and watched for an opening,
A word for my Master to say,
Ere the twilight gave place to darkness,
And the week had died away;
I knew that there had been moments
Afforded me through the week,
When I might have witnessed for Jesus,
But I hadn't the heart to speak,
And now, when I would have spoken,
The privilege was denied,
So I went in my sorrow to Jesus,
'And why is this?' I cried.

Ah! The Master knew all about it,
So He said, and I knew it was right,
'The tool is too blunt for service,
I cannot use it tonight.'
Oh, Christian, learn well this lesson,
We can only be used by God,
When communion with Him has fashioned
Our mouths like a sharpened sword;
The shaft to be used must be polished,
Must be hid in the Master's hand,
The arrow while hid in the quiver,
Must be sharp to perform His command;
Then polish and sharpen me, Master,
Though painful the process may be,
And make me an instrument fitted
To be used any moment by Thee."

As Unto Him

"When you think, or speak, or read, or write,
When you sing, or walk, or seek for delight,
To be kept from all wrong when at home or abroad,
Live always as under the eyes of the Lord.

Whatever you think, never think what you feel
You would blush, in the presence of God, to reveal;
Whatever you speak, in a whisper or clear,
Say nothing you would not like Jesus to hear.

Whatever you read, though the page may allure,
Read nothing unless you are perfectly sure
Consternation would not be seen in your look,
If God should say solemnly, 'Show Me that book!'

Whatever you write, though in haste or in heed,
Write nothing you would not like Jesus to read;
Whatever you sing, in the midst of your glees,
Sing nothing His listening ear would displease.

Wherever you go, never go where you'd fear
God's question being asked, 'What doest thou here?'
Turn away from pleasures you'd shrink from pursuing,
If God should look down and say, 'What are you doing?' "

Printed in the United States of America